A SPIRITUAL APPROACH TO MALE/FEMALE RELATIONS

QUEST BOOKS

are published by
The Theosophical Society in America,
a branch of a world organization
dedicated to the promotion of brotherhood and
the encouragement of the study of religion,
philosophy, and science, to the end that man may
better understand himself and his place in
the universe. The Society stands for complete
freedom of individual search and belief.
In the Theosophical Classics Series
well-known occult works are made
available in popular editions.

Cover design by Kathy Miners

A SPIRITUAL APPROACH TO MALE/FEMALE RELATIONS

Edited by Scott Miners

*This publication made possible with
the assistance of the Kern Foundation*

The Theosophical Publishing House
Wheaton, Ill. U.S.A.
Madras, India/London, England

The Theosophical Publishing House
306 West Geneva Road
Wheaton, Illinois 60187

Library of Congress Cataloging in Publication Data

(A Quest book)
"A Quest original" — T.p. verso.
Includes bibliographical references.
1. Sex — Religious aspects — Addresses, essays, lectures.
I. Miners, Scott, 1948-
BL65.S4S68   1984   291.1'78357   83-40236
ISBN 0-8356-0583-3 (pbk.)

Printed in the United States of America

for
K. A. M.

Contents

Contents

Contributing Authors

ROBERTO ASSAGIOLI, M.D., was born in Venice, Italy, in 1888 and took his medical degree at the University of Florence. He began pursuing psychological and philosophical studies while a medical student. Dr. Assagioli developed a new and comprehensive technique of psycho-therapy, called Psychosynthesis, in which the spiritual levels of awareness are integrated with the emotional and mental. He founded the Institute of Psychosynthesis in Rome in 1926. Later he became chairman of the Psychosynthesis Research Foundation, a non-profit educational corporation established to foster and support research in the field of psychology in regard to psychosynthesis. The psychosynthesis movement is spreading and growing in popularity. Dr. Assagioli published several hundred essays and articles and is also the author of *The Act of Will*.

CLAUDE BRAGDON was an architect, designer, writer, and stage designer. He is perhaps best known for the railroad station in Rochester, New York, which he designed. He counted among his friends Alfred Steiglitz, Georgia O'Keefe, Lewis Mumford, Theodore Roscoe, and Tennessee Williams, whose writing Bragdon influenced. He authored many

books, among which are *The Beautiful Necessity,
Old Lamps for New, The Ancient Wisdom in a
Modern World, Eternal Poles, New Image, Merely
Players, Introduction to Yoga, Yoga for You,* and
More Lives than One, his autobiography.

GINA CERMINARA, Ph.D., is author of many books, several of
which deal with the philosophy of Edgar Cayce.
These include *The World Within, Many Mansions,
Many Lives, Many Loves,* and *Edgar Cayce Re-
visited.* One of her most recent books, *Insight for the
Age of Aquarius,* is concerned with the impact of
General Semantics on our life style. The author re-
ceived her Ph.D. from the University of Wisconsin
and has also studied at the University of Rome, the
Wisconsin Conservatory of Music, and at the
Institute of General Semantics.

HARIDAS CHAUDHURI, Ph.D., was a disciple of Sri Aurobindo
and was president-founder of the California Institute
of Integral Studies, San Francisco, California. His
works included books and papers on the integral
psychology and philosophy derived from Sri Aurobindo's teachings, among which are *Mastering the
Problems of Living; Integral Yoga; Being, Evolution,
and Immortality;* and *The Evolution of Integral
Consciousness.*

CLARA CODD was active in the Women's Suffrage Movement
in England. Before her death in 1971, she authored
many books including *The Ageless Wisdom of Life*
and *Trust Yourself to Life.* She was a national
lecturer for the Theosophical Society in England,
which led to her becoming an international lecturer
for about sixty years. She was also past president of
the Theosophical Society in Australia and South
Africa.

VIKTOR E. FRANKL, M.D., Ph.D. is Professor of Neurology and Psychiatry at the University of Vienna Medical School and Distinguished Professor of Logotherapy at the United States International University (San Diego). Dr. Frankl is the author of twenty-six books that have been translated into eighteen languages. The American edition of his *Man's Search for Meaning* has sold over two million copies. Dr. Frankl has been visiting professor at Harvard, Southern Methodist, Stanford, and Duquesne Universities. Among other works in English by Dr. Frankl are *The Unheard Cry for Meaning, The Unconscious God, The Will to Meaning,* and *Psychotherapy and Existentialism.*

HERBERT V. GUENTHER, Ph.D., born in 1917, holds doctoral degrees from the universities of Munich and Vienna. He taught in India from 1950 to 1963 and became head of the Department of Comparative Philosophy and Buddhist Studies at the Sanskrit University in Varanasi in 1958. Since 1964 he has been head of the Department of Far Eastern Studies at the University of Saskatchewan in Canada. Among some of his books are *The Life and Teachings of Naropa* and *The Tantric View of Life.*

ELISABETH HAICH teaches yoga in Switzerland, where she started several yoga schools and is the co-director of the Yesudian Haich Yoga Center in Ponte Tresa, Tessin. She is the co-author of numerous books on yoga including *Yoga and Destiny.* She is also author of *Sexual Energy and Yoga* and *Initiation.*

HAZRAT INAYAT KHAN, the great Sufi mystic, lectured and taught in the West from 1910 until his death in 1927. He left a large number of unpublished lectures, which were collected and published in a twelve volume series titled *The Sufi Message of Hazrat*

Inayat Khan. His son, Pir Vilayat Khan, is now the head of the Sufi Movement.

CASI KUSHEL, M.F.C.C., is a psychotherapist in private practice in Berkeley, California. She is on the faculty at the California Graduate School of Marital and Family Therapy and was formerly an associate staff member in the Human Sexuality Program at the University of California, San Francisco.

J. KRISHNAMURTI was born in 1895 near Madras, India and studied in England. Now in his eighties, he continues to lecture worldwide on the theme of inner freedom through awareness of one's conditioning. The Trust bearing his name has founded schools in many countries for the purpose of "creating a new human being" free from aggression, competition, or comparison. From time to time Krishnamurti teaches at his schools, which extend to university level. Many books have been produced from his talks, among which are *Commentaries on Living (three volumes), First and Last Freedom, You are the World, Flight of the Eagle* and *The Impossible Question.*

GEDDES MACGREGOR LL.D., Ph.D., is Emeritus Distinguished Professor of Philosophy of the University of Southern California and the author of over twenty books. He was born in Scotland and became a naturalized U.S. citizen after coming to America in 1949 with his wife and two children, where he was the first holder of the Rufus Jones Chair of Philosophy and Religion at Bryn Mawr. He was Visiting Fellow at Yale in 1967-68 and has been Visiting Professor at various American and Canadian universities. He has also been special preacher at many famous churches, including St. Giles', Edinburgh, Princeton University Chapel, St. Paul's and Westminster Abbey, London, and he has lectured and preached widely in Europe and Asia.

JOHN MACMURRAY, LL.D., was born in Scotland, 1891, and died in 1976. He graduated with M.A.s from the University of Glasgow and from Oxford University and eventually received the honorary degree of LL.D. from the University of Glasgow. After holding other appointments, he became Professor of Moral Philosophy at the University of Edinburgh. His books include *Reason and Emotion, The Structure of Religious Experience, Challenge to the Churches, Persons in Relation,* and *Search for Reality in Religion.*

SCOTT MINERS is managing editor of *The American Theosophist,* the monthly journal of the Theosophical Society in America. He studied law at Western State University, College of Law of San Diego and is currently working toward a degree in religious studies. He is married and the father of one son.

SRI M. P. PANDIT is secretary of the Sri Aurobindo Ashram in Pondicherry, India. He is a world-recognized authority on yoga and the Indian spiritual tradition. He has written or edited more than eighty books on the teachings of Sri Aurobindo and the Indian spiritual legacy, his latest being *The Yoga of Love.* He is an authoritative exponent of Sri Aurobindo's yoga and ancient classical texts such as the Vedas, Upanishads, Tantra and the Gita. He has lived and practiced this yoga for almost forty years in Sri Aurobindo ashram under the direct guidance of Sri Aurobindo and the Mother.

SWAMI SIVANANDA RADHA is the founder and president of the Association for the Development of Human Potential in the United States. She is also the founder and

spiritual director of the Yasodhara Ashram, a yoga
retreat and study center in Canada. She received her
training at Sivananda Ashram in Rishikesh, India.
She is the author of *Kundalini: Yoga for the West*
and *The Divine Light Invocation.* Currently much of
her time and energy go into the workshop and
lecture tours.

DANE RUDHYAR has done pioneering work in formulating a
humanistic (and more recently, transpersonal) approach to astrology. He is the author of many books
on philosophy, metaphysics, the arts, and astrology.
Among these are *An Astrological Mandala, The
Planetarization of Consciousness, Occult Prepara-
tions for a New Age, The Astrology of Personality,
Astrological Timing,* and *Culture, Crisis and
Creativity.* In addition, he is a noted composer who
pioneered new tonal ideas in the '20s.

PITIRIM A. SOROKIN, Ph.D., received the Magister's degree
in criminal law and Doctor of Sociology from the
University of St. Petersburg, Russia, where he became Chairman of the Department of Sociology.
Later he came to the United States and joined the
faculty of the University of Minnesota. In 1930 he
became Chairman of the Sociology Department at
Harvard University. Under an endowment from the
Lilly Foundation, he established the Harvard Research Center in Creative Altruism, which was in-
corporated as the Research Society in Creative
Altruism. His list of published works includes thirty-
odd volumes which have been translated into many
languages. Among these are *The Ways and Power of
Love, The American Sex Revolution,* and *Social and
Cultural Dynamics.*

RENÉE WEBER, Ph.D., received her doctorate at Columbia
University and is Professor of Philosophy at Rutgers
University. She has authored articles on esoteric

and comparative East-West philosophy, on Plato, and on healing, many of which have appeared in *Main Currents in Modern Thought*, *Re-Vision*, *The American Theosophist*, and in various anthologies. She has published interviews and dialogues with well-known scientists in *The Holographic Paradigm and Other Paradoxes*, edited by Ken Wilber, and elsewhere.

JAY G. WILLIAMS, Ph.D., Professor and Chairman of the Department of Religion at Hamilton College, New York, is a specialist in the philosophy of religion. He is the author of *Yeshua Buddha* (1979), which is an interpretation of New Testament theology, and *Judaism* (1981), the story of the Jewish people, both published by the Theosophical Publishing House, Wheaton, Illinois.

Acknowledgments

The editor wishes to thank the following for their permission to reprint material:

Aurora Press for "Sexual Energy and Yoga" by Elisabeth Haich, in *Sexual Energy and Yoga*. Reprinted by permisson of the publisher.

Gina Cerminara for "Sex in the Edgar Cayce Readings," which was excerpted from her books *The World Within*, William Sloan Associates, Publisher, and *Many Lives Many Loves*, DeVorss and Company, 1963.

Faber and Faber Publishers for "Reason and Emotion" by John Macmurray. Reprinted by permission of Faber and Faber Ltd. from *Reason and Emotion* by John Macmurray.

Victor Gollancz Ltd., for "On Sex" by J. Krishnamurti. Reprinted from *The First and Last Freedom* by J. Krishnamurti. Copyright by Victor Gollancz Ltd., London.

Harper and Row, Publishers, Inc., also for "On Sex" by J. Krishnamurti. Chapter 21, "On Sex" from *The First and Last Freedom* by J. Krishnamurti. Copyright, 1954, by K&R Foundation, Inc. Reprinted by permission of Harper & Row, Publishers, Inc.

Alfred A. Knopf, Inc. for "The Worship of Eros" by Claude Bragdon from *Delphic Woman: Twelve Essays*, by Claude Bragdon. Copyright 1936 by Claude Bragdon and renewed 1964 by Henry Bragdon. Reprinted by permission of Alfred A. Knopf, Inc.

Main Currents in Modern Thought for "The Mysterious Energy of Love" by Pitirim Sorokin. *Main Currents in Modern Thought*, September, 1958.

Servire Publishers for "Passion" by Hazrat Inayat Khan. Reprinted from *The Sufi Message of Hazrat Inayat Khan*, by Hazrat Inayat Khan, Servire Publishers, p. 162. By Permission of Servire Publishers.

Shambhala Publications, Inc. for "The Male-Female Polarity in Oriental Thought" by Herbert V. Guenther. Reprinted by special arrangement with Shambhala Publications, Inc., 1920 13th Street, Boulder, Colorado 80302. From "The Male-Female Polarity in Oriental and Western Thought," by Herbert V. Guenther in *Maitreya 4: Woman* ©1973 by Shambhala Publications, Inc.

The Sterling Lord Agency, Inc. for "Transmutation and Sublimation of Sexual Energies" from *Psychosynthesis: A Manual of Principles and Techniques* by Roberto Assagioli, M.D., reprinted by permission of The Sterling Lord Agency, Inc., copyright ©1965 by Psychosynthesis Research Foundation.

Synthesis for "The Depersonalization of Sex" by Viktor Frankl. Reprinted with permission from *Synthesis 1, The Realization of the Self*, ©1974, 1977, by the Psychosynthesis Institute of the Synthesis Graduate School for the Study of Man, 3352 Sacramento St., San Francisco, California, 94118.

The Theosophical Publishing House Ltd., London, for

"Another Side of Sex" by Clara Codd. Reprinted from *The Creative Power* by Clara Codd and originally titled "The Esoteric Side of Sex," by permission of the Theosophical Publishing House, Ltd., London.

The Theosophical Publishing House, Wheaton for portions of the chapter "Wisdom in Human Relations" by Haridas Chaudhuri. Reprinted from *Mastering the Problems of Living* by Haridas Chaudhuri, by permission of the Theosophical Publishing House, Wheaton. Copyright 1968 by Haridas Chaudhuri.

Preface

There was a time in my life when I began to question some of the values I subscribed to concerning sexuality. I realized that I had become stuck in a pattern that had been established by peer pressure and socio-economic-group enculturalization.

As I began to question the meaning of sexuality (biologically, philosophically, and personally) I began to realize how little I knew. I looked into psychological, physiological, and philosophical books on sex and sexuality and found much useful information—some of which is included in this book. However, I could not find any one book that treated the subject in the meaningful way I wanted. Therefore, I started this project and looked for authors and articles that placed sexuality within the context of love, responsibility, and spiritual growth. The result is this compilation of articles from many points of view, which hopefully provides material that will help toward an understanding of the role of love and sex for conscious growth in daily life. My feeling is that this limited treatment of the subject will help in some way to an understanding of male and female attraction and put it in a new perspective for anyone not familiar with the viewpoints that follow.

I would also here like to thank the many people who gave me a helping hand or pat on the back. First I would like to thank my wife Kathie for her many extra hours of baby-sitting our son Christopher in his infant stage. Then many thanks are also due to Leonie Van Gelder, Mike King, Paul Hudson, Rosemarie Stewart, John Sameluk, Mary Jo Schneider, Jerry Rosser, Helen Bee, and, even though technically I am not supposed to thank her here, Shirley Nicholson of TPH for her support and editing help.

Introduction

Attraction between males and females is a familiar feeling. This physical polarity is one of the most obvious features of our lives. Yet, its very commonness too often obscures its uniqueness. Because it is so common, we tend to lose sight of the beauty and mystery of this oppositeness.

Popular interest in, and exploitation of, the relations between men and women has tended to emphasize biological or physical sex. We tend to forget that emotional, mental, and spiritual dynamics also play a part in these relations, and that constant multidimensional changes also take place between two people in a relationship. Nevertheless, there has always been an interest, though not so popular, in other dimensions of male/female relations. Why are there two sexes? Why is there attraction between them? Why have males exhibited characteristics, generally speaking, different from females? How does one express love in a relationship?

Sex is an important aspect of our lives, but it is frequently discounted, misused, and even mistrusted. By becoming more aware of this force we will be able to work with it more consciously and thus more creatively. At work, in the home, at play or leisure, life can become more meaningful by a recognition that this very personal attraction comes from an impersonal energy in the universe, which we sometimes glibly term "love."

Aligning oneself with this love, with its impersonality and palpable reality, can be a first step toward improving all our human relations. Its most obvious guise as an attractive force between the sexes serves as a graphic reminder that this love energy pervades our lives and all our relations.

This work is a compilation of articles that link love, spirituality, and sexuality. Most of the articles evidence perennial values and principles that extend from ancient traditions. These values have endured the forces of social, psychological, political, and cultural change, and they remain as goals for us to continue to pursue.

The book is arranged in three sections. The first focuses upon a social-cultural or human relations milieu. The second section deals primarily with metaphysical viewpoints, and the third has a religio-philosophical or even yogic flavor. There is some overlapping among the sections, and therefore each section has its own short introduction, which aims at distilling what is to follow.

Part I

Love Relationships

This section is an examination of the energy of love in relationships and as emotional sincerity. Love emerges not as a plaything of the immature but as a force to be reckoned with, a sacred aspect of life, just as knowledge is considered sacred by many seers and sages. It is seen as a character builder that can propel us both to greater self-awareness and to self-lessness.

The authors in this section examine human love in its right accommodation—a mature and sacralized expression. It has been secularized in our culture because it has been misunderstood, taken advantage of, and relegated to a place where it is too often taken for granted.

Our attitude toward love and a sagacious expression of it are related to the problem of dealing with sexual urges, an enigma confronting people of all cultures. What follows is an examination of human sex consciousness and clear guiding principles for its expression. This consideration of sex as it appears in the mind or thought and the motivation for its expression is woven throughout the articles, and always the mind of love—compassionate, mature, considerate love—is elevated to the seat of dominion over sex passion.

*To master the stuff he is made of—not to beat it into a
repressed subjection, not to make it into a singular god
to be worshipped—is what man needs to do as he lives
his wholeness in body as well as in spirit.*
Elizabeth B. Howes, Sheila Moon,
Man the Choicemaker

ROBERTO ASSAGIOLI

Transmutation and Sublimation of Sexual Energies

The problem of sex, the problem of how to deal in a sane and constructive way with the sexual drive, has confronted humanity ever since the beginning of civilization. But, for various reasons, this problem has now become more compelling, and public awareness of it is more acute; to use a current phrase, humanity has become definitely sex-conscious.

The crisis in the relations between the sexes is not isolated, but forms part and perhaps can be said to be the outstanding aspect of the general crisis which is deeply affecting the very foundations of existing civilization.

The authority of the religious and moral principles on which our civilization was based, the rules and customs which were formerly taken for granted and accepted (even if not always consistently applied) have lost or are rapidly losing their prestige, their binding and regulating power; even more, the younger generation is actively, and at times violently, revolting against them. The main cause of this crisis has been the fact that, while the religious fervor and the unquestioned acceptance of the theological and moral conceptions of the past have been rapidly losing their grip, the older and rigidly orthodox groups have attempted by sheer authority to enforce the strict rules, condemnations and prohibitions based on those theological and moralistic foundations.

Thus, in the past, in the sexual domain an attitude prevailed which led public opinion to regard the biological instincts and the human passions as bad and impure. Therefore, the method enjoined for dealing with them was that of suppression, except when the sex urge could find a justified satisfaction in lawful marriage. The whole subject of sex was considered improper, and adults tried to keep young people ignorant about it as long as possible.

The weakening of the religious influence on which that attitude was based, and the realization of the injurious effects of that suppression on health and character, evoked various movements of revolt. First we had the "return to nature," advocated by Rousseau and his followers; then the glorification of feeling by the romantic movement; later, revival of the hedonistic and aesthetic ideas of ancient Greece and the Renaissance, followed by the wave of philosophical and practical materialism, and the individualistic revolt against society and its norms as portrayed by Ibsen. Perhaps more important in modern society has been the influence of Freud and his followers of the psychoanalytic movement, which emphasized the psychopathological effects of sexual repression. All these concurred to foster and justify the uncontrolled gratification of all drives and impulses, the letting loose of every passion, the following of every whim.

But the result of this "liberation" did not produce the expected satisfaction and happiness. While it eliminated some of the drawbacks of the earlier rigid attitude and the consequent suffering, it produced other complications, conflicts and misery. The followers of uncontrolled sexual expression found, and are still finding, that excesses are necessarily followed by exhaustion or disgust; that the sexual drive and passion, even when not checked by moral considerations, cannot always find gratification owing to lack of suitable partners. Moreover, various drives often come into conflict with each other, so that indulgence in one requires the inhibition of another. For instance, a reckless yielding to sexual urge is apt to clash with self-preservation, creating a conflict between, for instance, lust and fear of disease. Further, an exaggerated sense of self-assertion may be in conflict with social mores and the consequent fear of the risks involved.

The lack of any stable guiding principle, of any clear scale of values, makes the individual insecure, robs him of self-reliance, and subjects him to the influence of other people and external circumstances. Moreover, ethical and spiritual principles or aspirations cannot be eliminated as easily as many seem to believe; they persist in the unconscious owing to hereditary and environmental influences, and also exist latent in the true spiritual nature of man. When violated, they arouse conscious or unconscious protest and consequently intense inner conflicts.

For clarity's sake the picture of the situation has been over-simplified. In reality we are at present in a period of transition, of confusion and of cross-currents. In some places and groups the old conditions persist; old concepts and methods are still being enforced. In many cases a state of violent reaction and of conflict between the generations prevails. In the more advanced and enlightened circles the exaggerated nature of the reaction has been recognized and attempts are being made to find and adopt balanced views and sound methods.

It is apparent that neither of the two extreme attitudes can give satisfactory results. One might think that some compromise between the two could be the way out of the impasse, but while such a common-sense procedure might avert the worst results of those extremes, experience indicates that it cannot be considered a satisfactory solution.

However, there is another alternative, a more dynamic and constructive way of handling the problem. This is based on, and takes advantage of, a fundamental property of biological and psychological energies, namely, the possibility of their *transmutation*—a possibility existing in all energies.

The real nature of the process is not well known, but such is the case with all "ultimates." For instance, it cannot be claimed that we have grasped the essential nature of electricity, but we know enough about its manifestations and the laws regulating them to enable us to utilize electricity in many diverse and often complicated ways, as in electronics. It is the same in the psychological field; we need not ascertain the ultimate nature of the psychological energies and their transmutations in order to utilize them increasingly through a growing knowledge of the laws that govern them and by means of appropriate and efficient methods based on those laws. We can therefore proceed confidently in our examination of the methods to be followed in the utilization for constructive ends of surplus or excessive sexual drives. This is particularly valuable, for instance, in balancing the sexual appetites of man and wife in marriage, or adjusting to situations where normal sexual relations are not available.

The first rule is to adopt an objective attitude toward sex, free from the traditional reactions of fear, prudishness, and condemnation, as well as from the lure and glamor—often artificially fostered—by which it is generally surrounded at present.

The sexual drive, like any other, is in *itself* neither "bad" nor "good." It is a biological function and, as such, it is not "immoral" but *pre*-moral. It has a great importance because it ensures the continuity of the animal species and of the human race. In animals it is subject to natural cyclic self-regulation. In civilized humanity it has become complicated through its close association with psychological functions, such as emotion and imagination, and with social and ethical factors which have partly over-stimulated, partly inhibited it. Therefore, the objective scientific attitude toward the sexual drive should be twofold: we should, on the one hand, eliminate the fears and condemnations, which have the effect of repressing it into the unconscious, as psychoanalysis has demonstrated; and, on the other hand, we should exercise a calm but firm control, followed by an active process of transmutation whenever its natural expression is unwarranted.

The processes of psychological transmutation and sublimation are symbolically indicated—although in obscure and abstruse ways—in the writings of alchemists (Jung, 9b). Other hints can be found in the works of writers on asceticism, such as Evelyn Underhill. In the modern approach to the subject we find the following significant statement by Freud: "The elements of the sexual instinct are characterized by a capacity for sublimation, for changing their sexual aim into another of a different kind and socially more worthy. To the sum of energies thus gained for our psychological productions we probably owe the highest results of our culture." (Freud: *Ueber Psychoanalyse*, Leipzig und Wien, Deutike, 1910, pp. 61-62).* This statement is important, for in it Freud himself shows the fallacy of considering the physical and instinctive aspects of sexuality separately and independently from its emotional and other psychological aspects. Yet this fallacy is committed by some investigators having a materialistic bias. Such a purely zoological consideration is altogether one-sided, and while those investigators have piled up a huge

---

*Many other psychologists have recognized the process of sublimation and dealt with it more or less extensively. Among them are Havelock Ellis (5), McDougall (11) and Hadfield (7). An accurate survey of the subject with many quotations and bibliographical references has been made by J. Trevor Davies in his book *Sublimation* (1917) (3). The theoretical problems and the differences of opinion aroused by the subject do not prevent—in this as in other cases—effective use of the process of psychological transmutation.

mass of facts, the neglect of their vital connection with the psychological aspect of sex, which is the truly *human* one, vitiates the conclusions drawn from them. James Hinton wittily remarked over half a century ago that to deal with the great fact of sexual love merely from the physical side would be like thinking, during a concert by Sarasate, of the cat's bowels and the horse's tail used in making the violin strings and bow (Ellis, 6).

In seeking to define the nature of sexuality we find in it three principal aspects:

1. A sensual aspect: physical pleasure.

2. An emotional aspect: union with another person.

3. A creative aspect: the birth of a new creature.

This classification does not claim to be scientifically accurate, but constitutes a practical aid in the process of transmutation. Each of the aspects mentioned can be transmuted or sublimated in accordance with its own specific nature.

Moreover, transmutations can take place in two directions. The first is the "vertical" or inward direction. Many instances of this kind of sublimation are offered by the lives and writings of the mystics of all times, places, and religions. Their autobiographies furnish most interesting evidence of the nature of this process, its crises and vicissitudes, the suffering it entails as well as the joys which reward its stress and strain. All of them speak of the "bliss" they experience—which, however, they regard as a possible hindrance if one becomes attached to it. One can also observe the different steps leading from human love to love for a higher Being, such as the Christ; this is the sublimation of the emotional aspect. They aspire to union with the Christ within, and some of them speak of it as the "mystical marriage." In psychological terms one would say that the goal of spiritual synthesis is the union of the personality with the spiritual Self, the first representing the negative feminine pole, the other the positive masculine pole. This polarity is a reality and not just a simple symbolical trans-position of a biological fact. It is one of the fundamental aspects of the spirit-matter polarity and is, so to speak, its reflection on the psycho-spiritual level, as sexual polarity is its expression on the physical level.

Let us pause here for a moment in order to dissipate certain confusions and misunderstandings that might arise. While the process of transmutation and sublimation can frequently be observed, one must not infer therefrom that *all* spiritual love is "merely" the outcome of sublimated sex, that it is possible to "explain away" a higher psycho-logical or spiritual manifestation by attributing its origin to biological sources or drives. The true nature of mysticism cannot be considered, as some investigators have main-tained, to be merely a product or by-product of sex. On the one hand, one finds many people whose normal sexual life is inhibited yet who show no trace of mysticism; on the other hand, there are instances of people leading a normal sexual life, raising a family, etc., and having at the same time genuine mystical experiences.

The spiritual life and consciousness belongs to a definite psychological level and has a quality which is specific and not derived. The transmuted energies reach up to it from below, as it were, and give it added vitality and "heat," but they neither create nor explain that higher life. The creative aspect can be sublimated in this "vertical" direction in the formation of a new regenerated personality. The growth of the "inner man" calls for these creative energies, and in accordance with the degree to which the individual employs them new spheres of action of increasing vastness will open up before him.

The second direction of the transmutation process is "horizontal" or external. Here also we find three kinds of transmutation, corresponding to the three aspects. The first, rather than being actual transmutation, consists of the substitution of other pleasures of the senses for sexual pleasure, from simple enjoyment of food to the enjoyment of contact with nature and to aesthetic pleasures by the cultivation of the appreciation of beauty through sight and hearing. The second consists of an enlargement or extension of love so as to include a growing number of individuals; the third produces or fosters artistic and intellectual activities.

When the physical sexual expression of human love is blocked for some reason, its emotional or feeling manifestations can be enhanced and reach a high level of ideal, "platonic" love. Further, independently of any obstacle to the free and complete expression of love, a gradual process of transmutation takes place normally and spontaneously in harmoniously married couples. At the beginning, the sexual and intensely emotional manifestations of love generally predominate, but in the course of years and decades this passionate aspect cools off and is transmuted into tender feeling, increasing mutual understanding, appreciation, and inner communion.

The love-energy derived from sexual sublimation can and does expand beyond love of one individual. It extends in concentric circles or spheres, encompassing ever larger groups of human beings. In the form of compassion it is poured upon those who suffer; then it undergoes a further transmutation and becomes a motive power for social and philanthropic action. Sublimated love-energy can also be expressed as comradeship and friendship for those with whom we have a common basis of understanding, aims and activity. Finally, it can reach out further until it radiates as brotherly love upon all human beings and upon all living creatures.

The third kind of transmutation of the sexual energies is into creative activities of an artistic or intellectual nature. The following statement by a great philosopher, Arthur Schopenhauer, strongly bears out this point:

> In the days and in the hours in which the tendency to voluptuousness is stronger . . . just then also the higher spiritual energies . . . are apt to be aroused most strongly. They are inactive when man's consciousness has yielded to lust, but through effective effort their direction can be

changed and then man's consciousness is occupied, instead of with those lower and tormenting desires, by the highest activities of the mind.

There appears to be a deep similarity between sexual energy and the creative energies operating at other levels of the human being. Artistic creation offers a particularly suitable channel for sublimation, and many instances can be found in the lives of great artists, writers, and composers. One of them, which has a special significance, is that of Richard Wagner. As is well known, he was at one time passionately in love with a married woman, Mathilde Wesendonck, to whom he gave music lessons and in whom he found an understanding of and a devotion to his genius which he missed in his first wife, Minna. After a short time they resolved to renounce the consummation of their love, and Wagner left Zurich and went, or rather fled, to Venice. At first his desperate mood induced ideas of suicide, but soon he set himself to write both the libretto and music of *Tristan and Isolde*, and in a kind of creative frenzy, completed the opera within a few months. During this period he wrote many letters to Mathilde and kept a diary intended for her. These were published after his death and in them one can clearly trace the gradual cooling off of his passion as he gave expression to it in the poetry and music of his opera. The completion of the work found him so detached that he wrote to Mathilde in a rather tepid and much lighter vein, and even paid her a short visit on purely friendly terms. That Wagner was aware of this process of sublimation and consciously fostered it is evident from a letter to Liszt: "As in my life I have never enjoyed the true happiness of love, I want to raise a monument to this most beautiful of all dreams, in which this love shall be fully satisfied, from beginning to end. I am planning a 'Tristan and Isolde.' "

Transmutation and sublimation is a process that can be either spontaneous or consciously and deliberately fostered and brought about. In the latter case, there is ample scope for the effective application of the facts and laws ascertained or rediscovered by modern dynamic psychology, and for the use of active techniques based on them. Here are some practical methods for such applications:

1. A firm conscious *control* of the drive to be transmuted, in which, however, care should be taken to avoid any condemnation or fear of it, as this could result in its repression in the unconscious. Non-condemnation of the drive, as such, does not imply a lack of realization of one's serious responsibility for the consequences, both individual and social, of its unregulated expression. Control can be helped by simple physical means, such as brisk muscular activity and rhythmic breathing; but the most effective, and at the same time the higher, way of controlling both the sexual and the power drives is the acceptance and recognition of every human being as a "Thou" to be respected, and not as an "object" for the gratification of our pleasure, an "it" to be dominated and exploited. The reality of such a basic "right relation" to our fellowmen and our duty to recognize it have been convincingly expounded and emphasized by Martin Buber (2).

2. The active release, development, and expression of the various aspects of personal and spiritual love—love for one's mate; love for others, beginning with those close to one and expanding to include increasing numbers of human beings in ever-widening circles and "upward" toward God or the Supreme. The emphasis should be put on the *expression* of love—in understanding and cooperation in altruistic and humanitarian activities.

3. The deliberate projection of one's interest, aspiration, and enthusiasm toward some *creative work* into which all one's energies can be poured. Various techniques for creative expression can be used for this purpose, such as drawing, writing, movement (Assagioli, 1).

4. The use of *symbols*. These exercise a strong attractive power on all our energies, conscious and unconscious, and specifically foster the process of transmutation.

Jung in his *Contributions to Analytical Psychology* (9) went so far as to state: "The psychological machinery which transmutes energy is the symbol." There is a great variety of symbols having an anagogic (uplifting) influence that can be made to serve this process, of which ideal human figures or "models" constitute an important class. Two types of these ideal figures, different and in a sense opposite, are respectively suited to men and women. A man may visualize some hero or a human-divine Being, such as the Christ, or he can use the image of an ideal woman like Dante's Beatrice or the Madonna. Inversely a woman can take as a model the highest type of womanhood her imagination can conceive or an image of the ideal Man. The influence of such "images" is beautifully expressed in the Indian saying: "Ganga (the sacred river) purifies when seen and touched, but the Holy Ones purify when merely remembered."

A simple and effective symbol is the lotus plant which transmutes the mud and water of the pond into the delicate substance and beautiful form and hue of its flower. This it does through its own inherent vitality and through the life-giving energy of the sun's rays. Desoille in his therapeutic method of the guided day-dream (4a) has made use of symbolic movement upward for the purpose of sublimation and transformation. Kretschmer (10) has summarized various techniques of imagery which can be used to foster this process of sublimation.

Other anagogic symbols may be produced spontaneously in dreams and in free drawing; Jung and his followers (E. Harding (8), F. Wickes (13) and others) have made an extensive study and application of them.

5. Close psychological *communion* with individuals or groups who have realized, or are striving to realize, the same aim. As there are chemical catalysts, so there are "human catalysts," whose influence, radiation, and the "atmosphere" they create, greatly facilitate psychological transformations.

The importance and value of transmutation and sublimation—not only of the sexual energies but of all other drives—should be more widely known and appreciated, and the methods for putting them in operation should be more extensively applied in psychotherapy, education, and self-actualization.

The process of transmutation and sublimation may be compared to the regulation of the waters of a great river, which prevents recurring disastrous inundations or the formation of unhealthy marshes along its banks. While a portion of the water is permitted to flow freely to its natural destination, the remainder is diverted through proper channelling to appropriate mechanisms that transform its energy into electricity to be employed as motive power for industrial and other purposes. In a parallel way, the conscious or unconscious drives, which produce so much individual suffering and social disturbance, can become, if rightly controlled and channelled, the springs of activities having great human and spiritual value.

REFERENCES

1. Assagioli, R.: "Creative Expression in Education," *American Journal of Education*, 1963, No. 1.

2. Buber, M.: *I and Thou*, New York, Scribners, 1958.

3. Davis, J. Trevor: *Sublimation*, London, Allen & Unwin, 1947. New York, Macmillan, 1948.

4. Desoille, R.: *Exploration de l'affectivité subconsciente par la méthode du rêve éveillé. Sublimation et acquisitions psychologiques.* Paris, D'Artrey, 1938.

4a. Desoille, R.: *Le Réve éveillé en psychothérapie*, Paris, Presses Universitaires de France, 1945.

5. Ellis, H.: *Little Essays of Love and Virtue*, New York, Doubleday, 1962.

6. Ellis, Mrs. H.: *Three Modern Seers: Hinton, Nietzsche and Carpenter*, London, Stanley, 1910.

7. Hadfield, J. A.: *Psychology and Morals*, London, Methuen, 1923. New York, McBride, 1925.

8. Harding, M. E.: *Psychic Energy. Its Source and its Goal*, New York, Pantheon Books 1947.

9. Jung, C. G.: *Contributions to Analytical Psychology*. New York, Harcourt Brace 1928.

9a. Jung, C. G.: *The Integration of the Personality*. London, Kegan Paul, Trench Trubner, 1940. New York, Farrar & Rinehart, 1939.

9b. Jung, C. G.: *Psychology and Alchemy*. Collected Works, Vol. 12, London, Kegan Paul, 1953. New York, Pantheon, 1953.

10. Kretschmer, Jr., W.: *Meditative Techniques in Psychotherapy*. (translated by Wm. Swartley). New York, Psychosynthesis Res. Found., 1959.

11. McDougall, W.: *The Energies of Men*. London, Methuen, 1932. New York, Scribner, 1933.

12. Sorokin, P. A.: *The Ways and Power of Love (Types, Factors and Techniques of Moral Transformation)*, Boston, Beacon Press, 1954.

13. Wickes, F. G.: *The Inner World of Man*. London, Methuen, 1950. New York, H. Holt, 1948.

2

> Give freedom to the ones who dwell close to your
> heart, not by separating yourself from them, trying to
> draw apart, for that often holds them in closer bonds.
> Give freedom in every thought, give love, overflowing
> love—with no restriction in your mind, no question of
> any kind.
>
> Elise Morgan, Your Own Path

CASI KUSHEL

Sexuality: A Consideration of Context

Human sexuality is an intricate and mysterious dance. For
most of us, the significance of this dance is not the physical
release alone, but a complex interaction of physical,
spiritual, and interpersonal needs. It is the quality of our
sexual experience, the nature of our relationships, our self
image and the meaning of our lives that provide the context of our sexuality.

As a family therapist with special training in the area of
human sexuality and sexual dysfunctioning, I am witness
to hundreds of stories of sexual dissatisfaction and frustration. Many people I see focus on some missing experience
or perceived lack of expertise. They blame their problems
on imagined physical inadequacy or dysfunction.

Most of these difficulties have nothing to do with any
real physical dysfunction. They are the product of misin-

formation, misunderstanding, repressed anger, poor communication skills, poor self image, feelings of inadequacy in other areas of life, lack of other meaningful interaction in the couple relationship, or unreal expectations. They are exacerbated by considering the sexual experience outside of the context of the relationship within which it exists and as separate from the quality of the rest of life.

As long as we are raised to view sexuality as removed from its proper context in our lives, we will experience confusion, dissatisfaction, and a sense of personal inadequacy in our sexual identity. We remain out of step with the dance.

In beginning to develop an integrated sexual identity we must recognize that sexuality takes place in a relationship, not in a void. It is an essential part of what Martin Buber calls the "I and Thou" relationship. It is our response to another, an expression of excitement and love.

We must begin to confront our sexuality as an expression of oneself to another or as an act of unity, part of loving and being loved. Further, we must reconsider the role of sexuality in procreation and as the bond which unites the parent couple over years of child raising. Our culture would benefit from addressing sexuality as Pir Vilayat Khan does —as "the energy of the race, something superpersonal."

If as a culture we treated sexual feelings as an expression of our enormous capacity to love, our miraculous ability to procreate and our enduring quest to transcend the mundane and experience the godlike nature of each of us, issues of sexual dysfunction would be rare. Children would be raised to feel pride in their sexual identity and adults would direct their sexual energy toward building healthy families and sharing loving feelings.

Since our earliest learning about ourselves in relationship to others and our first sexual feelings take place in childhood, let us consider how our sexual identity is formed in the family. It is the family that gives us our first sense of proper sexual context and molds our self image. It is the proper place to communicate the importance of feelings and the quality of experience which will later be generalized to sexual interaction. It is in the home that the spiritual component of sexuality is introduced.

Our sexual development begins with our earliest experiences of being touched as infants. If we are held often, caressed, treated with affection and respect, we begin to develop a sense of ourselves as lovable, valued, and secure in the world. That is the beginning of our sexual identity.

Even before we are born and wrapped in a blue or pink blanket, we are being prepared for our sexual future. The parents' attitudes toward the conception, pregnancy and birth experience will color the baby's first hours. As the baby explores his or her body, discovering fingers, toes, mouth and genitals, the parents' reactions will be recorded in the silent vocabulary of the babies' sexual responses. The information will be stored for future use, much of it unconscious and unremembered.

How the family communicates with each other or remains silent about sexual issues is another important ingredient in the development of a healthy sexual identity. A recent study (1978) of 1400 families in Cleveland, Ohio, confirmed the experience of sex counselors all across the United States. Between 85 and 95 percent of the parents in the study had never discussed any aspect of sexual behavior and its social consequences with their children. How can these children hope to be able to communicate to their loved ones when the time comes? How will they learn to share the feelings of sex?

As children grow, they notice whether or not their parents are comfortable touching each other and themselves. They are patterned by the fact that mothers touch and hold their little girls more than their boy children. They learn quickly if mother or father is ashamed of sexual body parts. They observe the respect and caring or lack of it that their parents show each other. All these aspects affect how children regard their male or femaleness and their developing sexuality.

Perhaps it seems too simplistic to make note of all these

ordinary things, but our self-concepts grow out of our daily interactions with other people—especially our interactions with our parents who are our first important others.

By the time children start school and must deal with outside information and peer pressure, they are already well on their way to becoming the sexual adults they are going to be. That is, most of their values and attitudes about themselves and how they will relate to others sexually are formed. If they have been taught to value and respect themselves, they will enter the larger world well-prepared to maintain that attitude.

If they have been led to believe that their genitals are shameful or that the process which brought them life is dirty and degrading, they will be easy prey to feelings of guilt, inadequacy, and shame. What is ironic is that those children are more vulnerable to misinformation and sexual misconduct than children who like and respect themselves.

Further, those children raised in families with a spiritual component report as adults they have better, more satisfying, sexual interactions than adults who were raised without a spiritual family life. These children were exposed to all the dirty words on bathroom walls, the Hollywood type of pornography that abounds and the larger than life movie stars' sex lives, but they had support, information and good modeling from their families. They also were given a sense of the spiritual component of sexuality. They see themselves whole and connected to all other creatures. They respond to sexuality as an extension of their spirituality and the mechanism that renews their love for a significant other.

This did not protect them from the self-doubt and awkwardness of adolescence. Each of those children on their way to adulthood and mature love passed through unrequited passions, temptations, rejections, and peer pressure to conform to sexual attitudes that were not in their best interest. What made these children later turn up on the top of a set of statistics that rated them the most satisfied with their sex lives, was the strong, positive self image with which they began the journey, and the love, support, and availability of their families along the way.

A more positive self image, developed with the love and support of their family in the context of a loving relationship, may lead to concern with how to enrich their family life, encouraging the budding sexuality of their children, and exploring their own potential to create transcendent experiences with people they love.

If we are to raise healthy, functional children with strong feelings of self-worth, we must become conscious of our own attitudes to sex in general, and our own sexuality in particular. We must consciously educate them with accurate information, model caring in our intimate relationships, encourage affection and respect in our families, take pride in our own bodies and in theirs, and be loving and demonstrative with them.

Perhaps, most importantly of all, we must encourage them to understand sexuality as a creative force, an opportunity to express their sense of oneness with another, a unity experience. Demonstrate the spiritual aspect of sexuality in your own life. Make it a part of your family experience. Share with them Martin Buber's vision of sex as a means by which love could be reborn. A sense that saw that love and sex need each other to realize both body and spirit. A vision that sex can be transcendent and erotic love, a divine dance.

3

*To love means . . . to subordinate oneself to the forma-
tion of a new subject, a "we." This depends . . .
upon the resolution of two subjects to accept life's
most difficult task, the creation of a double subject,
a "we," with complete disregard for egocentricity, all
prejudices, training formulas, and drives. He who has
enough courage so to love finds in living with his partner the strongest positive experience imaginable—the
appearance of super-personal purposes.*

Fritz Kunkel, Let's Be Normal

HARIDAS CHAUDHURI

Wisdom in Human Relations

EMOTIONAL IMMATURITY

The most baffling impediment to the deepening of love is
emotional immaturity. It consists of the inability to survive
the weather changes of love. Love as a human relationship
has its four seasons of spring, summer, autumn, and winter.
Spring is the honeymoon period. Summer is the period of
fulfillment. Autumn is the period of decline, the period of
growing misunderstanding and disenchantment. Winter is
the period of mounting resentment and mutual recrimination. When love survives all these seasonal changes, it dis-
covers a solid core of stability. When two individuals
discover that they have the same purposes in life, that they
have an abiding interest in the welfare of each other, and
that they can sink their differences for the sake of their

common cause, then no unfavorable wind can tear up their relationship.

During the springtime of love there is mutual enchantment. There is an upsurge of the positive forces of love. All differences and disconcerting features are thrown into the background or driven underground. A sort of hypnotic spell is created. The elemental urges, the fundamental psychic needs to love and be loved, assert themselves in an overwhelming measure. During the summer of love the newly found relationship reaches its climax and fulfillment. Partners bask in the sunshine of the love that has been realized, in the warmth of the actualized dream.

But then comes the autumn, when the spell begins to wear off and the process of disenchantment sets in. The clay feet of the idol of love are laid bare. The shadow side of personality begins to draw attention. The drawbacks and shortcomings which were submerged in the high tide of mutual admiration show up. The leaves of mutual attraction start falling. Immature love falls therewith.

An immature lover needs a perfect idol, a god, as an object of love. The exuberance of his love impulse can easily deify a suitable person, concealing feet of clay. As soon as the clay feet are revealed, the impulse evaporates and utter frustration follows. But when there is an irrepressible fund of psychic energy, it may proceed to create other god-like idols, one after another, each one to be demolished in due time. Under such conditions love can never strike deep roots.

It is emotional immaturity which gives force to the lure of novelty. An immature love relationship lasts so long as the feeling of novelty endures. With the sense of novelty worn out, love declines. The craving for novelty quickly responds to a new attraction. But it does not take long for the new love to be relegated to the limbo of oblivion. A person who is guided in his choice of friends by the lure of novelty or the glamor of perfection ends up being all alone and lovelorn. Even if he may not mean to reject old friends, friends naturally reject him sooner or later. Friendship is not a thing to be acquired and then taken for granted. It is rather like a living plant that has to be watered regularly, or a flame that has to be fed to keep it burning.

Emotional immaturity engenders hypersensitivity. It does not understand that every human being has his own problems, his own changing moods, his area of privacy, the sanctity of which must be respected. When a person is in a disturbed mood or is preoccupied with an emergent situation, he may naturally fail to respond in his usual manner or with his characteristic warmth and attention to the call of a friend. But if that friend happened to be hypersensitive, he would be quick to jump to conclusions. He would perhaps misconstrue the situation in terms of withdrawal of love. He might even impulsively react with anger and withdrawal on the basis of his hasty conclusion without any attempt to investigate and understand the specific circumstances of the situation.

Immaturity has no grasp of the essence of love as a relationship between two spiritual beings. Consequently it injects into human relations either the instinct of possessiveness and domination, or the policy of appeasement and overindulgence. When an immature person bestows his love upon another individual, he begins to feel that his love is a precious gift to which a high price tag has to be attached. He becomes demanding and exacting. He begins to expect more and more. The gift of his love is believed to confer upon him a property title. He wants to treat his love object as his private property or as a sphere of his sovereign control. He can brook no privacy or area of independence on the part of the person he loves. When love assumes this form, the winter season sets in upon one's emotional life. It heralds the beginning of mutual resentment and recrimination. The weaker party begins to feel suffocated under the tyranny of love. He gets ready to free himself from the golden yoke. He cannot tolerate any longer the profanation of his inner being.

In the contrary case, immaturity represents love as total appeasement. It is believed that in order to love, one must allow the beloved to do as he pleases. To please the object of love by all means becomes the sole concern of the lover. It is such immature love that creates the overindulgent lover. It creates the oversubmissive and mutely suffering wife. It also creates the politician who follows the policy of appeasement in the hope of making friends all around. He sacrifices principle to unreasonable demands. But in the long run such a policy does not pay. The overindulgent mother ruins the future of her child. The oversubmissive wife degrades her husband. The overappeasing politician encourages his enemy to turn into an insatiable tyrant. And eventually the relationship is degraded, if not destroyed.

During the winter season of love, the cold drafts of immature relationship begin to blow freely. The hate component of love comes to the front. Hitherto concealed drawbacks of the partners begin to loom large. Little lapses are magnified beyond proportion. Small unpleasant incidents become occasions for bitter argument and bickering. Tempest-in-a-teapot situations multiply. Mutual recriminations rise in a crescendo. When the only bond between two partners is a passing advantage or an impulsive infatuation or a legal contract, the rigors of winter can indeed deal the decisive death blow. But when the bond of relationship lies deeper, it may emerge out of the winter ordeal stronger and more stable.

There can be no abiding human relationship without the warmth of heart and genuine concern for each other. Love can exist without law, because it has a law of its own. As it grows it creates law and order. But divorced from love, law is a hollow thing. It smothers the spirit and turns life into a desert. So a too-legalistic attitude, for all its good intentions, is damaging to human relations. A moralist who is overenthusiastic in his devotion to abstract moral principles is neither effective in his reform nor helpful in his services. People expect from friends, first and foremost, not sermons but sympathy and love. In the absence of sympathy, sermons become repulsive. In the absence of love, ethical pronouncements sound like meaningless platitudes. They are too abstract and general and in consequence out of joint with the specific circumstances and problems that exist in a given situation. Love alone furnishes an insight into the specific nature of human situations. Love with its sympathetic understanding turns righteous indignation into gracious forgiveness. A self-righteous person likes to lift his voice in protest and criticism whenever he sees a flaw in human behavior or a falsehood in social life. He criticizes without any willingness to suffer and sacrifice. He is eager to reform without any understanding of the limitations of human nature. He fails to reform because he forgets to reform himself first. He loses more and more friends, turns friends into enemies, and finds himself impotent in the wilderness. The growing bitterness in his soul is reflected in the harshness of his judgment, and that harshness recoils upon him with ironic fury.

GUIDING PRINCIPLES OF HUMAN RELATIONS

Having discussed some of the roadblocks to satisfactory human relationships, we are now in a position to consider briefly some guiding principles. Here are two such principles: (1) delayed response; (2) spirit of accommodation.

Many of the blunders we commit in dealing with people are due to the habit of immediate and impulsive reactions. Having acted impulsively, we often regret later on and suffer irrevocably for spoiling a good relationship. You meet an impressive personality to whom you feel attracted. You are emotionally carried off to such an extent that you promptly concede to a request he makes without much thought, or make a promise or commitment, or confide to him a secret about yourself or a common friend. It is too late when you realize that you made a mistake. As you take steps to rectify the situation, you break your relationship with the person. If, however, you decide not to do anything about it, he spoils the relationship by making improper use of the secret you confided, or by taking undue advantage of the promise or commitment you made. In either case, irreparable damage has been done.

So there is a great need to tutor our unconscious minds not to behave impulsively and emotionally. The principle of delayed response is a useful one. When a critical decision is to be made, it is good to be able to think things over. It is in a cooler moment, when judgment is not swayed by impulse or emotion, that the right decision can be made. When confronted with an unexpected request or demand, it is good to be able to look at the matter from the distance of time instead of making a commitment right then and there. When involved in a provocative situation, it is wise not to respond instantly—and temperamentally. By losing his temper a person always weakens his own case and walks right into the trap of the enemy. Or perhaps he misconstrues the well-meaning criticism of a genuine friend and foolishly injures a beautiful friendship. In order to avoid such tragedies in human relationship, it is desirable to form the habit of delayed response. In dealing with people—friend, foe, or stranger—love and understanding have to be guided by reason so that impulse and emotion may not get the upper hand. Regular practice of meditation is a great help in such self-training. Meditation is the art of harmonizing the unconscious and the conscious. Through meditation, impulse and emotion are brought more and more into harmony with reason. And reason begins more and more to appreciate the importance of different impulses and emotions.

The spirit of accommodation is another guiding principle worthy of note. If he hopes to get along with people, a person cannot expect always to have his own way. If one expects others to fall in line with him, he must be ready to yield on occasion to their way, even though he may not like it. Human relationship is a two-way traffic. One has to give in, in order to earn the right to receive. One has to make concessions to others in order to gain their support and cooperation. With respect to such things as essential principles or common welfare or the ultimate goal, it is desirable to have the courage of conviction and an unyielding strength of character. But with regard to matters of minor importance, such as a choice between more or less convenient or expedient lines of action, it is good to feel the pulse of the people and accept the dominant tendency. He leads best who is led by the welfare of all concerned. He loves best who follows the love of all he is dealing with. The spirit of accommodation combines within itself the opposite qualities of strength and mercy, unflinching devotion and loving submission. Strength of character and devotion to principle prevent the spirit of accommodation from degenerating into rank opportunism. Loving concern for the welfare of all would make the spirit of accommodation an effective means of fruitful cooperation, and not a tactical device for self-glorification.

A clear understanding of the ultimate purpose of life and devotion to basic principles can stabilize love on a solid foundation. It is the spirit of love as free and joyful self-giving that can unite individuals on a permanent basis.

4

Love requires depth and loyalty of feeling; without them it is not love but mere caprice. True love will always commit itself and engage in lasting ties; it needs freedom only to effect its choice, not for its accomplishment. Every true and deep love is a sacrifice. The lover sacrifices all other possibilities, or rather, the illusion that such possibilities exist. If this sacrifice is not made, his illusions prevent the growth of any deep and responsible feeling so that the very possibility of experiencing real love is denied him.

C. G. Jung, Civilization in Transition

JOHN MACMURRAY

Reason and Emotion

A mutual sexual attraction is no proper basis for a human relationship between a man and a woman. It is an organic thing, not personal. What, then, is a proper basis? Love is, between any two persons. Love may or may not include sexual attraction. It may express itself in sexual desire. But sexual desire is not love. Desire is quite compatible with personal hatred, or contempt, or indifference, because it treats its object not as a person but as a means to its own satisfaction. That is the truth in the statement that doing what we want to do is not the same as doing what we ought to do.

But notice this—that mutual desire does not make things any better. It only means that each of two persons is treating the other as a means of self-satisfaction. A man and a woman may want one another passionately without either loving the other. This is true not merely of sexual desire but of all desires. A man and a woman may want one another for all sorts of reasons, not necessarily sexual, and make that mutual want the basis of marriage, without either loving the other. And, I insist, such mutual desire, whether sexual or not, is no basis of a human relationship between them. It is no basis of friendship. It is the desire to obtain possession of another person for the satisfaction of their own needs, to dare to assert the claim over another human being—"You are mine!" That is unchaste and immoral, a definite inroad upon the integrity of a fellow human being. And the fact that the desire and the claim are mutual does not make a pennyworth of difference. Mutual love is the only basis of a human relationship; and bargains and claims and promises are attempts to substitute something else; and they introduce falsity and unchastity into the relationship. No human being can have rights in another, and no human being can grant to another rights in himself or herself. That is one of the things of which I am deeply convinced.

Now take another point. There is only one safe-guard against self-deception in the face of desire, and that is emotional sincerity, or chastity. No intellectual principle, no general rule of judgment is of any use. How can a man or woman know whether they love another person or merely want them? Only by the integrity of his or her emotional life. If they have habitually been insincere in the expression of their feelings, they will be unable to tell. They will think they love when they only want another person for themselves. What is usually known as "being in love" is simply being in this condition. It blinds us to the reality of other people; leads us to pretend about their virtues, beauties, capacities, and so forth; deprives us of the power of honest feeling and wraps us in a fog of unreality. That is no condition for any human being to be in. If you love a person you love him or her in their stark reality, and refuse to shut your eyes to their defects and errors. For to do that is to shut your eyes to their needs.

Chastity, or emotional sincerity, is an emotional grasp of reality. "Falling in love" and "being in love" are inventions of romantic sentimentality, the inevitable result of the deceit and pretence and suppression from which we suffer. Love cannot abide deceit, or pretence or unreality. It rests only in the reality of the loved one, demands the integrity of its object, demands that the loved one should be himself, so that it may love him for himself.

In the second place, between two human beings who love one another, the sexual relationship is one of the possible expressions of love, as it is one of the possible co-operations in love—more intimate, more fundamental, more fraught with consequences inner and outer, but essentially one of the expressions of love, not fundamentally different in principle from any others, as regards its use. It is neither something high and holy, something to venerate and be proud of, nor is it something low and contemptible, to be ashamed of. It is a simple ordinary organic function to be used like all the others, for the expression of personality in the service of love. This is very important. If you make it a thing apart, to be kept separate from the ordinary functions of life, to be mentioned only in whispers; if you exalt it romantically or debase it with feelings of contempt (and if you do the one you will find that you are doing the other at the same time; just as to set women on a pedestal is to assert their inferiority and so insult their humanity): if you single out sex in that way as something very special and wonderful and terrible, you merely exasperate it and make it uncontrollable. That is what our society has done. It has produced in us a chronic condition of quite unnatural exasperation. There is a vast organisation in our civilization for the stimulation of sex—clothes, pictures, plays, books, advertisements and so on. They keep up in us a state of sexual hypersensitiveness, as a result of which we greatly overestimate the strength and violence of natural sexuality. The most powerful stimulant of sex is the effort to suppress it. There is only one cure—to take it up simply, frankly and naturally into the circle of our activities; and only chastity, the ordinary sincerity of the emotional life, can enable us to do so.

Sex, then, must fall within the life of personality, and be an expression of love. For unlike all our other organic functions it is essentially mutual. If it is to be chaste, therefore, it must fall within a real unity of two persons—within essential friendship. And it must be a necessary part of that unity. The ideal of chastity is a very high and difficult one, demanding an emotional unity between a man and a woman which transcends egoism and selfish desire. In such a unity sex ceases to be an appetite—a want to be satisfied—and becomes a means of communion, simple and natural. Mutual self-satisfaction is incompatible with chastity, which demands the expression of a personal unity already secured. Indeed, it seems to me, that it is only when such a unity in friendship has reached a point where it is shut up to that expression of itself that it is completely chaste. How can two people know that their love demands such an expression? Only through a mutual chastity, a complete emotional sincerity between them. That alone can be the touchstone of reality. And the law of reality in the relationship of persons is this: " 'the integrity of persons is inviolable.'You shall not use a person for your own ends, or indeed for any ends, individual or social. To use another person is to violate his personality by making an object of him; and in violating the integrity of another you violate your own." In all enjoyment there is a choice between enjoying the other and enjoying yourself through the instrumentality of the other. The first is the enjoyment of love, the second is the enjoyment of lust. When people enjoy themselves through each other, that is merely mutual lust. They do not meet as persons at all, their reality is lost. They meet as ghosts of themselves and their pleasure is a ghostly pleasure that cannot begin to satisfy a human soul, and which only vitiates its capacity for reality.

5

The lover asked his Beloved if there remained in Him anything still to be loved. And the Beloved replied that he had still to love that by which his own love could be increased.

Ramon Lull, The Book of
the Lover and the Beloved

J. KRISHNAMURTI

On Sex

Question: We know sex as an inescapable physical and psychological necessity and it seems to be a root-cause of chaos in the personal life of our generation. How can we deal with this problem?

Krishnamurti: Why is it that whatever we touch we turn into a problem? We have made God a problem, we have made love a problem, we have made relationship, living a problem, and we have made sex a problem. Why? Why is everything we do a problem, a horror? Why are we suffering? Why has sex become a problem? Why do we submit to living with problems, why do we not put an end to them? Why do we not die to our problems instead of carrying them day after day, year after year? Sex is certainly a relevant question but there is the primary question, why do we make

life into a problem? Working, sex, earning money, thinking, feeling, experiencing—you know, the whole business
of living—why is it a problem? Is it not essentially because
we always think from a particular point of view, from a
fixed point of view? We are always thinking from a center
towards the periphery but the periphery is the center for
most of us and so anything we touch is superficial. But life
is not superficial; it demands living completely and because
we are living only superficially we know only superficial
reaction. Whatever we do on the periphery must inevitably
create a problem, and that is our life: we live in the superficial and we are content to live there with all the problems
of the superficial. Problems exist so long as we live in the
superficial, on the periphery, the periphery being the 'me'
and its sensations, which can be externalized or made subjective, which can be identified with the universe, with the
country or with some other thing made up by the mind.

So long as we live within the field of the mind there must
be complications, there must be problems; that is all we
know. Mind is sensation, mind is the result of accumulated
sensations and reactions and anything it touches is bound to
create misery, confusion, an endless problem. The mind is
the real cause of our problems, the mind that is working
mechanically night and day, consciously and unconsciously. The mind is a most superficial thing and we have spent
generations, we spend our whole lives, cultivating the
mind, making it more and more clever, more and more
subtle, more and more cunning, more and more dishonest
and crooked, all of which is apparent in every activity of our
life. The very nature of our mind is to be dishonest, crooked,
incapable of facing facts, and that is the thing which creates
problems; that is the thing which is the problem itself.

What do we mean by the problem of sex? Is it the act, or
is it a thought about the act? Surely it is not the act. The
sexual act is no problem to you, any more than eating is a
problem to you, but if you *think* about eating or anything
else all day long because you have nothing else to think
about, it becomes a problem to you. Is the sexual act the

problem or is it the thought about the act? Why do you think about it? Why do you build it up, which you are obviously doing? The cinemas, the magazines, the stories, the way women dress, everything is building up your thought of sex. Why does the mind build it up, why does the mind think about sex at all? Why? Why has it become a central issue in your life? When there are so many things calling, demanding your attention, you give complete attention to the thought of sex. What happens, why are your minds so occupied with it? Because that is a way of ultimate escape, is it not? It is a way of complete self-forgetfulness. For the time being, at least for that moment, you can forget yourself—and there is no other way of forgetting yourself. Everything else you do in life gives emphasis to the 'me,' to the self. Your business, your religion, your gods, your leaders, your political and economic actions, your escapes, your social activities, your joining one party and rejecting another—all that is emphasizing and giving strength to the 'me.' That is, there is only one act in which there is no emphasis on the 'me,' so it becomes a problem, does it not? When there is only one thing in your life which is an avenue to ultimate escape, to complete forgetfulness of yourself if only for a few seconds, you cling to it because that is the only moment in which you are happy. Every other issue you touch becomes a nightmare, a source of suffering and pain, so you cling to the one thing which gives complete self-forgetfulness, which you call happiness. But when you cling to it, it too becomes a nightmare, because then you want to be free from it, you do not want to be a slave to it. So you invent, again from the mind, the idea of chastity, of celibacy, and you try to be celibate, to be chaste, through suppression, all of which are operations of the mind to cut itself off from the fact. This again gives particular emphasis to the 'me' who is trying to become something, so again you are caught in travail, in trouble, in effort, in pain.

Sex becomes an extraordinarily difficult and complex problem so long as you do not understand the mind which thinks about the problem. The act itself can never be a problem but the thought about the act creates the problem. The act you safeguard; you live loosely, or indulge yourself in marriage, thereby making your wife into a prostitute which is all apparently very respectable, and you are satisfied to leave it at that. Surely the problem can be solved only when you understand the whole process and structure of the 'me' and the 'mine': my wife, my child, my property, my car, my achievement, my success; until you understand and resolve all that, sex as a problem will remain. So long as you are ambitious, politically, religiously or in any way, so long as you are emphasizing the self, the thinker, the experiencer, by feeding him on ambition whether in the name of yourself as an individual or in the name of the country, of the party or of an idea which you call religion—so long as there is this activity of self-expansion, you will have a sexual problem. You are creating, feeding, expanding yourself on the one hand, and on the other you are trying to forget yourself, to lose yourself if only for a moment. How can the two exist together? Your life is a contradiction; emphasis on the 'me' and forgetting the 'me.' Sex is not a problem; the problem is this contradiction in your life; and the contradiction cannot be bridged over by the mind, because the mind itself is a contradiction. The contradiction can be understood only when you understand fully the whole process of your daily existence. Going to the cinemas and watching women on the screen, reading books which stimulate the thought, the magazines with their half-naked pictures, your way of looking at women, the surreptitious eyes that catch yours—all these things are encouraging the mind through devious ways to emphasize the self and at the same time you try to be kind, loving, tender. The two cannot go together. The man who is ambitious, spiritually or otherwise, can never be without a problem, because problems cease only when the self is forgotten, when the 'me' is nonexistent, and that state of the non-existence of the self is not an act of will, it is not a mere reaction. Sex becomes a reaction; when the mind tries to solve the problem, it only makes the problem more confused, more troublesome, more painful. The act is not the problem but the mind is the problem, the mind which says it must be chaste. Chastity is not of the mind. The mind can only suppress its own activities and suppression is not chastity. Chastity is not a virtue, chastity cannot be cultivated. The man who is cultivating humility is surely not a humble man; he may call his pride humility, but he is a proud man, and that is why he seeks to become humble. Pride can never become humble and chastity is not a thing of the mind—you cannot become chaste. You will know chastity only when there is love, and love is not of the mind nor a thing of the mind.

Therefore the problem of sex which tortures so many people all over the world cannot be resolved till the mind is understood. We cannot put an end to thinking but thought comes to an end when the thinker ceases and the thinker ceases only when there is an understanding of the whole process. Fear comes into being when there is division between the thinker and his thought; when there is no thinker, then only is there no conflict in thought. What is implicit needs no effort to understand. The thinker comes into being through thought; then the thinker exerts himself to shape, to control his thoughts or to put an end to them. The thinker is a fictitious entity, an illusion of the mind. When there is a realization of thought as a fact, then there is no need to think about the fact. If there is simple, choiceless awareness, then that which is implicit in the fact begins to reveal itself. Therefore thought as fact ends. Then you will see that the problems which are eating at our hearts and minds, the problems of our social structure, can be resolved. Then sex is no longer a problem, it has its proper place, it is neither an impure thing nor a pure thing. Sex has its place; but when the mind gives it the predominant place, then it becomes a problem. The mind gives sex a predominant place because it cannot live without some happiness and so sex becomes a problem; when the mind understands its whole process and so comes to an end, that is when thinking ceases, then there is creation and it is that creation which makes us happy. To be in that state of creation is bliss, because it is self-forgetfulness in which there is no reaction as from the self. This is not an abstract answer to the daily problem of sex—it is the only answer. The mind denies love and without love there is no chastity; it is because there is no love that you make sex into a problem.

6

If the desire to be honest is greater than the desire to be "good" or "bad," then the terrific power of one's vices will become clear. And behind the vice the old forgotten fear will come up (the fear of being excluded from life) and behind the fear the pain (the pain of not being loved) and behind this pain of loneliness the deepest and most profound and most hidden of all human desires: the desire to love and to give oneself in love and to be part of the living stream we call brotherhood. And the moment love is discovered behind hatred all hatred disappears.

Fritz Kunkel, In Search of Maturity

VIKTOR E. FRANKL

The Depersonalization of Sex

When we speak and think about love, we should remember that it is a specifically human phenomenon. We must see to it that it is preserved in its humanness, rather than treated in a reductionistic way. Reductionism is a pseudoscientific procedure which takes human phenomena and either reduces them to or deduces them from subhuman phenomena. Love, for example, is frequently interpreted in a reductionistic way as a mere sublimation of sexual drives and instincts which man shares with all the other animals. Such an interpretation blocks a true understanding of all the various human phenomena.

In fact, love is one aspect of a more encompassing human phenomenon which I have come to call *self-transcendence*.[1] By this term I wish to denote that being human always relates to and is directed toward something other than itself.

38

Man is not, as some current motivation theories would like to make us believe, basically concerned with gratifying needs and satisfying drives and instincts, and by so doing, maintaining, or restoring, homeostasis, i.e., the inner equilibrium, a state without tensions. By virtue of *the self-transcendent quality of the human reality* man is basically concerned with reaching out beyond himself, be it toward a meaning which he wants to fulfill, or toward another human being whom he wants to lovingly encounter. In other words, self-transcendence manifests itself either by one's serving a cause, or loving another person.

Loving encounter, however, precludes considering, and using, another human being merely as a means to an end. It precludes, for example, using a person as a mere tool to reduce the tensions aroused and created by libidinal, or aggressive, drives and instincts. Such an attitude toward one's partner, however, is a distortion of human sex.

This is due to the fact that *human sex is always more than mere sex*, and it is more than mere sex precisely to the extent to which it serves and functions as *the physical expression of something metasexual*, namely, the physical expression of love. And only to the extent to which sex carries out this function of an embodiment, an incarnation, of love—only to this extent is it also climaxing in a really rewarding experience. Thus, Maslow was justified when he once pointed out that those people who cannot love never get the same thrill out of sex as those people who can love. And among those factors which contributed most to enhancing potency the highest ranking, according to 20,000 readers of an American psychological magazine who had answered a pertinent questionnaire, was romanticism, that is to say, something that comes close to love.

Of course, it is not quite accurate to say that only human sex is more than mere sex. As Irenaeus Eibl-Eibesfeldt[2] has evidenced, in some vertebrates sexual behavior serves group cohesion, and this is particularly the case in primates that live in groups; thus, in certain apes sexual intercourse sometimes exclusively serves a social purpose. In humans,

Eibl-Eibesfeldt states, there is no doubt that sexual inter-course not only serves the propagation of the species but also the monogamous relation between the partners.

But while love is a human phenomenon by its very nature, the humanness of sex is only the result of a developmental process—it is the product of progressive maturation.[3] Let us start with Sigmund Freud's differentiation between the *goal* of drives and instincts over against their *object*: one might say that the goal of sex is the reduction of sexual tensions whereas its object is the sexual partner. But as I see it, this only holds for neurotic sexuality. To the mature person the partner is no "object" at all; the mature person, rather, sees in him another *subject*, another *human being*, seeing him in his very *humanness*; and if he really loves him, he even sees in him another *person* which means that he sees in him his very *uniqueness*—and it is only love that enables a person to seize hold of another person in that very uniqueness which constitutes the personhood of a human being.[4]

Promiscuity is, by definition, the very opposite of a monogamous relation. An individual who indulges in promiscuity need not care for the uniqueness of a partner and therefore cannot love him. Since only that sex which is embedded in love can be really rewarding and satis-factory, the quality of the sexual life of such an individual is poor. Small wonder, then, that he tries to compensate for this lack of quality by the quantity of sexual activity. This, in turn, requires an ever more multiplied and increasing stimulation as is provided, for example, by pornography.

From this, one might understand that we are in no way justified in glorifying such mass phenomena as promiscuity and pornography by considering them as something pro-gressive; they are rather regressive; after all, they are symptoms of a retardation that must have taken place in one's sexual maturation.

We should not forget that the myth of sex-just-for-fun's-sake (rather than letting sex become the physical expres-

sion of something metasexual) as something progressive is
sold and spread by people who know that this is good business. What intrigues me is the fact that the young generation not only buys the myth, but also the hypocrisy behind
it. In an age such as ours in which hypocrisy in sexual matters is so much frowned upon, it is strange to see that the
hypocrisy of those who propagate a certain *freedom from
censorship* remains unnoticed. Is it so hard to recognize
that their real concern is *unlimited freedom to make money*?[5]

But there cannot be successful business unless there is a
substantial need that is met by this business. And in fact, we
are witnessing, within our present culture, what one might
call an *inflation of sex*. We can only understand this phenomenon against a comprehensive background. Today, we
are confronted with an ever increasing number of clients
who complain of a feeling of meaninglessness and emptiness, of an inner void, of the *existential vacuum*[6] as I am
used to calling it. This is due to the following two facts:
in contrast to an animal, man is not told by drives and instincts what he must do; and in contrast to man in former
times, he is no longer told by traditions and values what he
should do. In our day, he sometimes no longer knows what
he really wishes to do.

It is precisely this existential vacuum into which the
sexual libido is hypertrophying. And it is precisely this
hypertrophy that brings about the inflation of sex. As any
kind of inflation, e.g., that on the monetary market, sexual
inflation is associated with de-valuation. And sex is devaluated inasmuch as it is dehumanized. Thus, we observe
the present trend to living a sexual life which is not integrated into one's personal life, but rather lived out for the
sake of pleasure. The *depersonalization of sex* is understandable once we diagnose it as a symptom of what I call
existential frustration: the frustration of man's search
for meaning.[7]

So much for causes; but what about the effects? The more
one's search for meaning is frustrated, the more such an

individual embarks on what since the American Declaration of Independence has been termed the "pursuit of happiness." In the final analysis, the pursuit is intended to serve the purpose of intoxication and stupefaction. But, alas, it is the very pursuit of happiness that dooms it to failure. *Happiness cannot be pursued because it must ensue*, and it can ensue only as a result of living out one's self-transcendence, one's dedication and devotion to a cause to be served, or another person to be loved.

Nowhere else is this general truth more perceptible than in the field of sexual happiness. *The more we make it an aim, the more we miss it.* The more a male client tries to demonstrate his potency, the more he is likely to become impotent; and the more a female client tries to demonstrate to herself that she is capable of fully experiencing, the more liable she is to be caught in frigidity. And most of the cases of sexual neurosis I have met in my many decades of practice as a psychiatrist can easily be traced back to this state of affairs.

Accordingly, an attempt to cure such cases has to start with removing that demand quality which the sexual neurotic usually ascribes and attributes to sexual achievement. I have elaborated on the technique by which such a treatment can be implemented, in a paper published in the *International Journal of Sexology* in 1952.[8] What I want to state here, however, is the fact that our present culture which, due to the motivation outlined above, idolizes sexual achievement, further adds to the demand quality experienced by the sexual neurotic, and thus further contributes to his neurosis. The use of the Pill, by allowing the female partners to be more demanding and spontaneous, has unwittingly encouraged the trend. American authors observe that the women's liberation movement, by having freed women of old taboos and inhibitions, has had as one result that even college girls have become ever more demanding of their sexual satisfaction, demanding it from college boys.[9] The paradoxical result has been a new set of problems variously called "college impotence" or "the new impotence."[*]

The Victorian sexual taboos and inhibitions are going, and to the extent that real freedom is gained, a step forward has been taken. But, freedom threatens to degenerate into mere license and arbitrariness, unless it is lived in terms of responsibleness. And that is why I do not tire of recommending that the Statue of Liberty on the East Coast be supplemented by a Statue of Responsibility on the West Coast.

---

[*]Konrad Lorenz has shown that it is not only in humans that the demand quality or—for that matter—sexual aggressiveness on the part of the female partner can result in impotence for the male; this also happens in animals. There is a species of fish whose females habitually swim "coquettishly" away from the males who seek mating. However, Lorenz succeeded in training a female to do the very opposite—to forcefully approach the male. The latter's reaction? Just what we would have suspected to be shown by a college boy: a complete incapacity to carry out sexual intercourse!

REFERENCES

1. Frankl, V. E., *Psychotherapy and Existentialism* (Washington Square Press, New York, 1967).

2. Eibl-Eibesfeldt, I., *Frankfurther Allgemeine Zeitung*, February 28, 1970.

3. Frankl, V. E., *The Doctor and the Soul* (Vintage Books, New York, 1973).

4. _____, *Man's Search for Meaning* (Pocket Books, New York, 1963).

5. _____, "Encounter: The Concept and Its Vulgarization," *The Journal of the American Academy of Psychoanalysis*, 1 (1973): p. 73.

6. _____, "The Feeling of Meaninglessness: A Challenge to Psychotherapy." *The American Journal of Psychoanalysis*, 32 (1972): p. 85.

7. _____, *The Will to Meaning* (New American Library, New York, 1969).

8. _____, "The Pleasure Principle and Sexual Neurosis," *The International Journal of Sexology*, 5 (1952): p. 128.

9. Ginsberg, G. L., Frosch, W. A. and Shapiro, T., "The New Impotence," Arch. Gen. *Psychiat.*, 26 (1972): p. 218.

> The American divorce rate has been variously at-
> tributed to teenage marriage, delayed marriage, pre-
> marital sexual experience, lack of sexual experience,
> decline of religious influence, residual puritanism,
> glamorization of divorce, and even the automobile.
> But our analysis suggests a different, perhaps a shock-
> ing answer: American marriages are unstable because
> Americans marry for love.
>
> Gail and Snell Putney

SCOTT MINERS

Divorce and Separation

Love between the sexes has been considered as an expression of divine love since the time of the Vedas, those
ancient and revered texts of India that date from 1500
years B.C. As suggested in the Vedic tradition, this world
we live in is a reflection, "an image of reality, the eternal,
infinite, unchanging One mirrored in the temporal, finite,
changing world." (Griffiths, 1982). All that takes place
within the world then must also exist in some way in that
One. The love that exists between men and women, parents
and children, friend and friend is an aspect of divine love.
The divine nature is thus seen as being all pervasive. That
is why love and sex have been viewed as reflections of
divine love, and I suggest it is the reason humans are able
to experience a deeper, more profound, even mystical love
—one where the human and divine meet. However, for

a healthy relationship, it is essential to expect to give this love rather than to receive it (Fromm, 1963).

A related concept used in the Hindu tradition is that there is no real separation: what appears to be separate is maya, or an illusory view. All things are interconnected. The forms we see are fluid, ever-changing maya. A relation, though terminated for all practical purposes, is kept alive at a deeper level, as it may live in the mind, in the emotions of the parties to it. In the yoga system of Patanjali the bundle of thoughts and actions accumulated in any relationship is termed karma. In Buddhism the term skandha describes the group of attributes that we carry with us. In either case this karma, as described by Patanjali, is made up of imprints that enter the unconscious by thoughts, acts, and emotions. They are said to unite at the birth of a human and constitute part of his or her personality (Taimni, 1968.) When these concepts are put together they indicate that a relationship takes place at more than the physical level.

This Eastern view also indicates that a human is transcended by something in life that is causative and immanent, a divine principle. It evokes a picture of a human as one who is a part of the divine in his innermost being. As the Hindu would say, Brahman (the Ultimate Reality) pervades all. Indeed, the most important aspect of the Eastern world view is awareness of the unity and interrelatedness of all phenomena in nature, human and other. Yoga in fact means union with this Reality, both in that we are already so united and that we must try to become aware of this union through yoga methods such as meditation. Thus arises the admonition of the Upanishad to love not so much the husband or wife as the divine within the husband or wife. In fact, it is said enlightenment can be reached through this relationship:

> As a man, when in the embrace of a beloved wife, knows nothing within or without, so this person, when in the embrace of the Atman, knows nothing within or without.
>
> Brihadaranyaka Upanishad. 4.3.21

It seems that many people today end relationships for what in retrospect seem minor reasons. Married people divorce over what initially was a minor conflict or a mere difference of opinion. Some have said that it is unfortunate that they divorced since they see later that they did so at a time when their judgment was unclear, when they were angered with one another or upset in some way. Admittedly marriage relationships are difficult. A humorist once wrote "for twenty years my wife and I were ecstatically happy . . . then we met." However, this splitting apart of married couples ultimately creates anxiety. There is a lack of understanding, there is hatred. Some run to others for support and talk about all the faults of their spouse, and anger builds. There are hurt feelings. When the parties do not resolve their conflict, it has an energy of its own that affects others as well as those directly involved. The concept of karma implies that the residual of the incomplete relationship continues to have an effect.

One remarkable aspect of divorce and multiple divorces is that people tend to assume that in the next marriage the partner will fulfill all their desires and needs. But, as Seikan Hasagawa points out, we should not devote so much time to picking out the best partner. Time should instead be spent in transforming the relationship into one where each person experiences conscious and spiritual growth. The partner should therefore be looked at as a trusted friend and not as an adversary (Hasagawa, 1977). The challenges, the obstacles, point to inadequacies in oneself and therefore to an opportunity to overcome fetters to growth.

Of course, sometimes it is better for people to go their separate ways. Many times a relationship can be too difficult for anyone to cope with. One needs to be reasonable about this and use common sense. It does not seem to be sensible to continue a relationship with someone who is mentally or physically cruel or who otherwise acts in an aggressive, hurtful way most of the time or with any degree of consistency. Nor is it reasonable to continue a relationship with someone who is not faithful. Here, however, the discussion will concern people who are interested in resolving their conflicts where reason declares this to be the prudent and desirable course of action.

COMPASSION

The root of the word *divorce* is "to divert," and a literal meaning is "to separate." In this sense, any time there is a separation, or a diverting, there is divorce. However, *divorce* today connotes the dissolution of a marriage, and this is usually due to some incompatibility between the partners that they feel is irresolvable. This form of dissolution takes place mostly on grounds other than compassion for the other person, though there are many cases where the parties mutually agree on all aspects of the dissolution.

Many separations take place, on the other hand, because of a feeling of animosity or intense dislike and hatred. This is very unfortunate because the effects of such behavior are damaging to others besides the married couple. When children are involved, their sensitive natures are hit by these strong emotions of their parents and, as they do not understand, they feel guilty and also lose their sense of self-confidence. If the partners could act from true compassion for others, this negative behavior would never arise in the mind and thus would never be expressed.

Because of the attraction between people of the opposite sex, there is a great deal of pleasure derived from and anticipated in the relationship. As George Bernard Shaw said (*Getting Married*): "When two people are under the influence of the most violent, most insane, most delusive, and most transient of passions, they are required to swear that they will remain in the excited, abnormal, and exhausting condition continuously until death do them part." This wry statement has an element of truth in it. One of the great stresses in married life comes when anticipated pleasure is not forthcoming. The partner comes to be seen as someone with whom there will be conflict, and conflict is not pleasurable. But if there is a general sense of compassion for others, and less of a feeling of ego-grasping or selfishness, it seems these minor conflicts can be resolved easily. However, they must be faced. They will not dissipate, except after long periods, unless they are resolved.

In one sense, compassion for others derives from being aware that everyone has many difficulties in life. There is no one who is completely happy all the time; some people are generally happier than others, but even their happiness is not lasting. As the Tibetan teacher Geshe Kelsang Gyatso said, when the fleeting state of happiness of others is seen, we realize that all humans ultimately must face many frustrations (Gyatso, 1980). There are many fears that must be resolved by everyone—fear of conflict, fear of not getting what is wanted, loss of pleasure, and even fear of death. If this is remembered, it can be easier to have compassion for others. If there is a conflict with the husband or wife, this sort of compassionate feeling can help resolve the conflict.

One can train oneself to react with compassion. However, just as a seed planted in the ground will not become a mature plant overnight, this requires some time. With practice, it just takes a moment of reflection, an instantaneous meditation to generate a feeling of compassion. This feeling will then affect how we handle situations. This notion of compassion is expressed beautifully in a Mahayana Buddhist sutra, (Suzuki, 1963):

> When an only son in a good family is sick, the parents feel sick too: when he is recovered they are well again. So it is with the Bodhisattva (enlightened one). He loves all sentient beings as his own children. When they are sick, he is sick too. When they are recovered, he is well again. Do you wish to know whence this (sympathetic) illness is? The illness of the Bodhisattva comes from his all-embracing love (mahakaruna).

Minor conflicts do not take on major proportions when we are motivated by this sort of compassion. There are many methods outlined in Mahayana Buddhist texts for the generation of compassion, far too many for the purposes of this paper, but at the foundation of all of them is the intent to be concerned about the well-being of others. Indeed, in this system one must pass through a long practice of smoothing the rough edges of one's nature before reaching the state of supreme Buddhahood (discovery of one's true Self). Interestingly, as our own attitude and reactions change, the other pole of the relationship, i.e., the spouse's, will also change. Again, however, the doctrine of karma has an important role here; that is, we reap what we sow.

The way to perfection is arduous. Karmic patterns and predispositions can be stumbling blocks. Much accumulation of merit is needed, as well as untiring personal effort to weed out the negative aspects of a personality. As the noted Buddhist scholar D. T. Suzuki points out (1963):

> This can be accomplished only through the karma of good deeds untiringly practised throughout many a generation. Each single act of goodness we perform today is recorded with strict accuracy in the annals of human evolution and is so much the gain for the cause of righteousness. On the contrary, every deed of ill-will, every thought of self-aggrandisement . . . is a drawback to the perfection of humanity . . . . Later Buddhism has thus elaborated to represent . . . the concrete results of good and evil karma, and tries to show in what direction its followers should exercise their spiritual energy.

ANGER

Perhaps one's own anger and that of the partner is the most difficult aspect of a relationship to face. Anger can be very dangerous. It is a destructive energy that can ruin relationships through violent external expression; if repressed it can destroy natural health. It clouds judgment and makes one repulsive to others.

Many people say that it is good to express anger. Perhaps this attitude is a reaction to the discovery that repressed anger is the cause of much ill health, both physical and psychological. It is most likely, however, that when anger is expressed it will only get stronger. The stoics held that when given in to, anger builds. Possibly their views were rooted in the Eastern notion that the samskara, or corresponding energy vortice in one's emotional field, is given more energy each time anger is produced and acted upon. Further, if anger is expressed, it will very likely provoke an angry reaction, and then two people will be angry with one another, which may cause many unfortunate consequences.

In their paper titled "Fields and their Clinical Implications," Dora Kunz and Erik Peper (1983) maintain that, whereas love is peaceful and tranquil and tends to elicit an energetic connection of openness between people, anger "is more likely to close and shut out the other person because the recipient tends to respond in the same way, and thus a barrier is formed." These authors then recommend "strategies to reduce the impact and expression of anger." When we feel anger arising, we can shift our attention to someone with whom we have a loving relationship. This may produce an affectionate warmth, and we can let this love flow out briefly. In that short process, we can see the cause of the anger more clearly and perhaps change our feeling toward the person with whom we are angry. This also allows us to see that we have an ability to decrease our own angry responses.

In this process there is no repression of the anger; it is admitted, recognized—we do not say "I am not angry" when in fact we are—and also there is no expression of the anger. Its energy dissipates as our emotions are changed from hostile to loving. This of course is a challenge. It is difficult to be compassionate and loving if someone is taking advantage of us, and in some cases perhaps one should not put up with this but should confront the injustice, while trying to maintain a compassionate mind.

If another person is angry, a good way to try to remain compassionate toward him or her is to remember a time when our own anger dominated our emotions. Someone angry with us really needs our compassion and patience, perhaps more than ever. If we return the anger, matters will only get worse. After the expression of anger we feel drained, clouded in judgment. But if we can shift our attention, the situation can be seen in a better perspective. We may be able to see that the angry person is in trouble of some sort.

It is difficult nonetheless not to react to someone else's anger. Sometimes we may need to reflect on the situation in a quiet place. It would be useful to use Kunz and Peper's technique again and think of someone for whom we have warm and loving feelings. This will help restore our emotions to a quiet, peaceful state. Then we can try to visualize the person whom we may resent. But if the image brings back a feeling of resentment, we should let it go and again imagine someone we love and let that feeling pervade us. We should repeat the visualization until we can see the person whom we resent in a new way, with a feeling of compassion. It is very helpful to learn to send love out deliberately to another. It generates a real energy and has an effect. One method for generating love and compassion was explored above—to see others as having only fleeting happiness in life, while at the same time having many frustrations and anxieties.

Anger and compassion are of course only two aspects of relationships. There are many others to explore, such as patience, unselfishness, altruism, and joy. However, anger and compassion are seminal aspects of any relationship, and a knowledge of the dynamics of these two basic emotions can prepare a solid groundwork for any lasting relationship.

ONE, NOT TWO

One whole governs the moving and the stable, that which walks and flies, this variegated creation.

                               Rig Veda III. 54.8

Perhaps one of the strongest notions held in the Christian world is the admonition of Jesus to "let no one put asunder what God has brought together." A corollary to this is the statement that the two will become as one. It is possible to see that no one can take apart what God has put together, that all life is one, and perhaps one valid interpretation of Jesus's statement is, "Do not think that you are separate from one another; when you act against another, you act against yourself; when you love another, you love yourself." It is not possible to act without affecting others. In a strong relationship many people sense a growing together, a becoming one, or an almost mystical feeling of unity. This is much like the statement in the Upanishad referred to earlier regarding loving the divine in the husband or wife.

The Sanskrit term advaita refers to the Hindu "not two." This conveys the concept that the universe is pervaded by a divine Immanence (Brahman). As we have seen, all seemingly unrelated things in the world are connected together by this Immanence, which is the ground of their being. This concept is mirrored in the Christian explanation of the Father in heaven, or the mystical Christ—the "Son" that pervades all, the tree of which we are the branches. In Buddhism, the term advaya refers to this same concept, "not two." The concept of one life, then, is universal, appearing in many religions.

What keeps us from seeing this one life? The ancient traditions say it is our selfishness. We wish to fulfill our own desires and are basically concerned with our own needs. Yet if we were to live as if the two were parts of the One, we would be more concerned for the well-being of others. We would be less attached to our close relationships, and we would see more clearly and compassionately the husband or wife.

By practicing methods for generating compassion and decreasing anger, we can help ensure that our close relationships will be happier. This experience will enable us to live more peacefully within and express love and compassion more universally as well.

REFERENCES

1. Fromm, Erik. *The Art of Loving.* New York: Bantam, 8th ed., 1963.

2. Griffiths, Bede. *The Marriage of East and West.* Springfield: Templegate, 1982.

3. Gyatso, Kelsang. *Meaningful to Behold: A Commentary on Shantideva's Boddhisattvacharyavatara.* Cumbria, England: Wisdom Publications, 1980.

4. Hasagawa, Seikan. *Essays on Marriage.* Los Angeles: J. P. Tarcher, 1977.

5. Kunz, Dora, and Peper, Erik. "Fields and their Clinical Implication, Part III—Anger and How it Affects Human Interactions." In *The American Theosophist,* June, 1983.

6. Suzuki, D. T. *Outlines of Mahayana Buddhism.* New York: Schocken, 1963, first published in 1907.

7. Taimni, I. K. *The Science of Yoga.* Wheaton: Theosophical Publishing House, Quest, 2nd ed., 1968.

8

All Come to me at last,
There is no love like mine;
For all other love takes one and not another;
And other love is pain, but this is joy eternal.
          Edward Carpenter, "Over the Great City"

PITIRIM A. SOROKIN

The Mysterious Energy of Love

I

In recent decades science has opened several new fields to its exploration and use. The probings into the subatomic world and the harnessing of atomic energy are but two examples of these ventures. Perhaps the latest realm to be explored is the mysterious domain of altruistic love. Though now in its infancy, its scientific study is likely to become a most important area for future research: the topic of unselfish love has already been placed on today's agenda of history and is about to become its main business.

Before the First World War and the later catastrophies of our time science largely shunned this field. The phenomena of altruistic love were thought to belong to religion and ethics rather than to science. They were considered good topics for preaching but not for research and teaching. Moreover, the prewar science was much more interested in the study of criminals than of saints, of the insane than of the genius, of the struggle for existence than of mutual aid and of hate and selfishness than of compassion and love.

The explosion of the gigantic disasters after 1914 and the pending danger of a new suicidal war have now radically changed the situation. These calamities have given impetus to the scientific study of unselfish love. They have also led to basic revisions of many theories until now regarded scientific, and especially those which dealt with the causes and means of prevention of wars, revolutions, and crime.

Among other things these revisions have shown that without reinforcement by the energy of unselfish love, all the fashionable prescriptions for elimination of these ills of humanity cannot achieve their task. This conclusion equally applies to all the prescriptions that try to prevent conflicts by either purely political, educational, sham-religious, economic, or military means. For instance, we may like to think that if tomorrow all the governments in the world were to become democratic, we would finally have a lasting peace and crimeless social order. Yet, recent careful studies of comparative criminality, of 967 wars and 1629 internal disturbances in the history of Greece, Rome, and the Western countries since 600 B.C. up to the present time show that democracies have hardly been less belligerent, turbulent, and crime-infested than autocracies.

The same goes for education in its present form as a panacea against international wars, civil strifes, and crimes. Since the tenth century on up to the present time education has made enormous strides forward. The number of schools of all kinds, the percent of literacy, and the number of scientific discoveries and inventions have greatly increased. Yet, the number and deadliness of wars, bloody revolutions, and grave crimes have not decreased at all. On the contrary, in this most scientific and most educated twentieth century they have reached unrivaled heights and have made this century the bloodiest in the past twenty-five centuries of Graeco-Roman and Western history.

Similarly, the tremendous progress of knowledge and domestication of all forms of physical energy has not given man any lasting peace. Rather, it has greatly increased his chances of being destroyed in all forms of interhuman conflicts.

Even shallow—purely verbalistic and ritualistic—religion does not help much in this task, if such an "easy" religion is not implemented by deeds of unselfish love. Jesus, St. James, and St. Paul quite correctly stated that "faith without works is dead," and that "in Jesus neither circumcision availeth anything, nor uncircumcision; but faith which worketh by love." As systematic practice of the commandments of love is much more difficult than a mere "verbalistic-ritualistic" profession of faith, the truly religious, who unfailingly practice their moral commandments, have always made up an insignificant minority of members of any religious group. Among millions of Christians there are few who regularly practice such precepts of the Sermon on the Mount as: "love your enemies, do good to them that hate you," "whosoever shall smite thee on thy right cheek, turn to him the other also," or most of the other precepts of this Sermon. The same is true of the followers of other religions with a multi-million membership. When we investigated 73 converts of a popular evangelist we found out that only one of these "mass-assembly line converts" had tangibly changed his overt behavior in an altruistic direction. This deep chasm between noble preachings and ignoble practices explains the modest results of religions in prevention of strife. As this chasm seems to have deepened during the last few centuries there is a little chance for the verbalistic religions to achieve this task in the future.

Finally, the same is to be said about other "magic" prescriptions for elimination of the deadly forms of social conflicts. Neither an establishment of the Communistic, or

Socialistic, or Capitalistic economies can accomplish this task because none of the historical societies with these types of economy have been free from this strife. No more hopeful are the beliefs in establishment of a lasting—international and internal—peace by the means of a "massive retaliation" by nuclear or other "ultimate" instruments of warfare. Practiced for millennia, this policy of "peace through power" or through the Roman *si vis pacem para bellum* (if you want peace, prepare for war) has not given to humanity even modestly long peace periods. Recent studies show that on average the incidence of war occurred every two to four years in the Graeco-Roman and Euro-American history, while the incidence of an important internal disturbance took place in about every five to seventeen years in these countries. Finally, the same studies disclose the fact that each time a more murderous means of warfare has been invented, the scale, the destructiveness, and the casualty of wars and revolutions have tended to increase, instead of decreasing. These "sinister" facts sufficiently well demonstrate the hopelessness of these policies for realization of a lasting peace.

To sum up: the unforgettable lesson given by the catastrophes of this century convincingly shows that without increased "production, accumulation and circulation" of the energy of unselfish love, none of the other means can prevent the future suicidal wars, nor can it establish a harmonious order in the human universe. The mysterious forces of history seem to have given man an ultimatum: perish by your own hands or rise to a higher moral level through the grace of creative love. This situation explains why a serious study of this energy is being started now, and why it is likely to become a most important field of research in the future.

II

　　"All this may be true," my skeptical friends often say to me, "but where are the proofs that this energy of love can work? And if so, how can we increase its production, accumulation, and circulation in the human world?" My answer to these difficult questions is as follows: Our extant knowledge of this energy is, so far, almost negligible. Our "know-how" of its efficient production and utilization is also very meager. And yet, this little knowledge and poor "know-how" warrant enough the hypothesis that this "grace of love" is one of the three highest energies known to man (along with those of truth and beauty).

This energy or power is different from, and irreducible to, the scaler quantities of physics called "force," "work," "power," and "energy." Its properties are qualitative rather than quantitative. As yet, we do not have any "unit" of this energy (like erg in physics) for its exact measurement. So far, we can only appraise very roughly when its (a) intensity, (b) extensity, (c) purity, (d) duration, and (e) adequacy are "notably greater or lesser." If these (a,b,c,d,e) are called "the dimensions of love," these "dimensions" are again different from the dimensions of "force" or "energy" in physics, expressed in the formulas: MLT^2 and ML^2T^2. We do not know, also, whether the law of conservation of energy and other principles of physics are applicable to the energy of love. The term "energy" is used here in its general meaning, as "ability to produce action or effect."

In human beings this energy operates in producing the diverse and complex inner experiences called empathy, sympathy, kindness, compassion, admiration, benevolence, reverence, affection, friendship, and love. In the world of human relations it appears in all situations where another person is treated as an end-value but not the means to any purpose. On a social plane love works in all interactions between two or more persons where one's valuable aims and aspirations are shared and helped (to come about) by other persons. Accordingly, all actions and relationships of this sort can be regarded as "workings" of love-energy in different degrees of purity, intensity, duration, and adequacy.

Potentially the energy of love is a tremendous—creative

and recreative—power. When it is better known, reverently treated, and wisely applied, it can substantially help in freeing mankind from its gravest ills: war, crime, insanity, misery and cussedness.

For the last few decades, biology, psychology, sociology, and other branches of science have steadily converged toward this view. Their rapidly increasing body of evidence shows, first, that the energy of love is indispensable for generation, continuity, and growth of living forms, for survival and multiplication of species, and for maintenance of health and integrity especially of human individuals. Thus, contemporary biology instructs us that without a minimum of cooperation and mutual aid between parents and the progeny neither multiplication nor survival of either unicellular or multicellular organisms is possible. This is particularly true in regard to human beings. The helplessness of the newly-born dooms him to certain death if he is not helped for several years of his childhood. The decisive role of heterosexual love in the procreation and raising of normal human beings needs only to be mentioned to show "the workings" of love-energy in this vital matter.

The phenomena of suicide disclose these "works" in their own way. The main factor of so-called "egoistic" and "anomique" suicide is the utter loneliness of its victim, especially when it is caused by sudden disruption of the victim's intimate social attachments. Those who are not loved by anyone and who do not love anybody are the first candidates for demise. The best prevention of it is, therefore, to break free from imprisonment within one's own shell through loving, and being loved by others.

The curative power of love manifests itself in many other ways. Today's psychosomatic medicine informs us that the combination of too little love with too much hate in a person is largely responsible for many cardiovascular, respiratory, gastrointestinal, endocrinologic, genito-urinary and skin diseases, plus for some forms of epilepsy and headache. A great surgeon, John Hunter, suffering from a heart ailment, well summed up this situation by saying, "My life is at the mercy of any rascal who can make me angry."

A rapid deterioration of the health of babies deprived of warm, motherly love is typically demonstrated by a careful, filmed study of what happened to such babies in a well-managed New York foundling home. After three months of separation from their mothers the foundlings began to lose their appetite, failed to sleep, and became shrunken, whimpering, and trembling. During the additional two months their deterioration increased. Twenty-seven babies died during the first year; seven more died during the second year. Twenty-one survived longer, but were so altered that thereafter they could be classified only as idiots. Except for motherly love, these babies had all the care and attention necessary for their well-being. And yet, lack of genuine love made these conditions insufficient to secure the foundlings' survival and healthy growth.

The grace of love—in both forms of loving and being loved—is necessary not only for survival and physical health of infants, but also for their growth into mentally and morally sound citizens. Now we know well that the bulk of juvenile delinquents and psychoneurotics is recruited mainly from the ranks of persons who in their early life were deprived of a minimum of love in their families and in their "unneighborly neighborhood." On the other hand, the Mennonite, the Hutterite, the Mormon and the Friends' communities in the United States yield either none or the lowest quota of criminals, mentally sick, drug-addicts, sex-perverts, and libertines. The main reason for this is that these brotherly communities not only preach love, but steadily practice it not only in regard to the members of their family, but to all members of their community, and even to all members of the human race.

The curative power of love is also increasingly emphasized by recent psychiatric research. It shows that the main healing agent in the treatment of mental disorders is not so much the specific technique of various schools of psychiatry as much as the establishment of rapport—of mutual sympathy and trust—between the therapist and the patient, and placing the patient in a social climate free from enmity and conflict. This possibly explains the "miracle" of healing of a large number of sick persons by the saintly apostles of unselfish love.

Being able to cure physical, mental, and moral sickness, love-energy also contributes to the prolongation of human life. This fact is typically illustrated by the longevity of some 4500 Christian saints studied. These saints lived in the first to the eighteenth centuries, when the average life-span was much shorter than it is in the United States today. Most of the saints lived in the conditions which, according to present standards of public health, were far from hygienic. Many of the saints were ascetics and deprived their bodies of the satisfaction of vital needs. In spite of these adverse conditions, their average longevity was as high, at least, as that of contemporary Americans. An abundant and pure love of the saints for God and for neighbors appears to be largely responsible for their outstanding longevity.

This conclusion is confirmed by the opposite, life-shortening, effects of hate and enmity also ascertained by many recent studies.

The total body of the existing evidence, illustrated by the preceding samples, hardly leaves any doubt of the highly beneficial biological functions performed by the energy of love in human life. Even in the evolution of species and in the behavior of living forms, including man and his social life, the role of mutual aid, cooperation, and other manifestations of this energy is now recognized by science to be as important, at least, as the role of the struggle for existence, which up to recent decades has been regarded as the main factor of the evolution of life and of the course of human history.

III

Besides these biological functions the energy of love

serves mankind in many other ways. Thus, it has worked—and can increasingly do so—as the best "extinguisher" of interhuman enmity and strife. For our experimental testing of this old truth, we took five pairs of students with a strong mutual dislike of the partners of each pair. We set a task to change in three months, by the technique of "good deeds," their inimical relationships into amicable ones. We persuaded one partner of each pair to begin to render to the other partner small deeds of friendliness, like an invitation to lunch, to the movies, to a dance, or an offer to help in home work, and so on. At the beginning these deeds were performed without enthusiasm on the part of the renderer, and a few times were rejected by the other partner. Being however repeated, they began to melt enmity and eventually replaced it with warm friendship in four pairs and by an "indifference" in the fifth pair. Similar experiments performed in the Boston Psychopathic Hospital between mutually hostile nurses and patients gave similar results.

Another experimental testing of the old motto "love begets love and hate begets hate" showed that in two experimental groups (of students and patients of a mental institution) the friendly approaches of the members of each group to one another brought forth friendly responses in 65 to 80 percent of cases, while aggressive approaches were answered by aggressive responses in about the same percent.

Our detailed investigation of how and why each of some 500 students studied happened to have a certain individual as his "best friend" and another individual as his "worst enemy" disclosed the fact that in almost all the cases of the best friend as well as of the worst enemy the friendship was started by some friendly action, while the enmity was engendered by an aggressive act, of one or of both of the parties.

Historical demonstration of the power of love in taming war and strife is typically illustrated by the policy of Emperor Asoka (c.264-226 B.C.). Horrified by "the abomination of desolation" wrought by his victorious wars,

Asoka, under the influence of Buddhism, in the second part of his life radically replaced his belligerent policy with one of peace, friendship, and amelioration of vital economic, mental, and moral conditions of his own people as well as of those in neighboring states. By this policy of "love begets love" he was able to secure peace for some seventy-two years. Considering that such a long period of peace happened only three times in the whole history of Greece, Rome, and thirteen European countries, Asoka's achievement strongly suggests that the policy of real friendship can secure a lasting peace more successfully than the policy of hate and aggression, unfortunately still followed by the governments of our time.

Generally, the pacifying power of love appears to be the main agency which terminates the long and mortally dangerous catastrophes in the life of nations. A systematic study of all such catastrophes in the history of ancient Egypt, Babylonia, China, India, Persia, Israel, Greece, Rome, and of the Western countries uniformly shows that all such catastrophes were finally overcome by a notably altruistic ennoblement of the people, culture, and social institutions of these nations. This ennoblement often emerges and spreads in the form of a new religion of love and compassion (like Buddhism or Jainism or Christianity), or as moral and spiritual enrichment of the old religion and its moral commandments. We must not forget that practically all the great religions emerged in catastrophic circumstances and, at their initial period, were first of all and most of all moral social movements, inspired by sympathy, compassion, and the Gospel of Love. They set out to achieve the moral regeneration of a demoralized society. Only later on did such movements become overgrown by complex theological dogmas and impressive rituals. This is equally true of the emergence and initial period of Confucianism, Taoism, Zoroastrianism, Hinduism, Jainism, Buddhism, the Mosaic and the Prophetic Judaism, Christianity, and other ethico-religious movements.

Love-energy not only increases the longevity of

individuals, but also the life-span of societies and organizations. Social organizations built mainly by hate, conquest, and coercion, like the Empires of Alexander the Great, Caesar, Ghengis Khan, Tamerlane, Napoleon or Hitler, have had, as a rule, a very short life—a few years, decades, rarely a few centuries. So it has been with various organizations in which unselfish love plays an unimportant role. Thus the average longevity of small economic establishments like drug, hardware, or grocery stores in this country is only about four years. Big business firms (listed on American and European stock exchanges) survive on average only about twenty-nine years. Even the longevity of most of the states rarely goes beyond one or two centuries. The longest existing organizations are the great ethico-religious bodies like Taoism, Confucianism, Hinduism, Buddhism, Jainism, Christianity, and Mohammedanism. All of these organizations have already lived for more than one thousand years—some for over two thousand, and there are no clear signs of their dissolution in the foreseeable future. The secret of their longevity probably lies in their dedication to the altruistic education of mankind and, generally, to the cultivation of love in the human universe.

Finally, the gigantic power of love is manifested in the undying influence of the greatest apostles of love upon the countless millions of human beings and on the course of human history. If we ask ourselves what kind of individuals have been most influential in human history, the answer is the persons like Lao Tze, Confucius, Buddha, Zoroaster, Mahavira, Moses, Jesus, St. Paul, St. Francis of Assisi, M. Gandhi, and other creators and leaders of altruistic religions and morality. Only, perhaps, the influence of the greatest scientists, inventors, philosophers, and artists— that is, of the creative geniuses in the fields of Truth and Beauty—can somewhat rival the beneficent influence of the great apostles of love. In contrast to the short-lived, and often destructive, influence of autocratic monarchs, military conquerors, revolutionary dictators, and potentates of wealth, the great apostles of love have most tangibly affected the lives, minds, and bodies of untold billions during the millennia of history, and still affect us. They had neither armed forces, nor wealth, nor any of the worldly means of influencing the course of history and destiny of nations. Though their bodies were not of the strongest, nor their I.Q.s of the highest, according to the standards of current mental tests, by the power of their pure and abundant love they accomplished the transformation of millions of men and women, reshaped cultures and social institutions, and conditioned the course of history.

The preceding sketch of the working of unselfish love shows that it is indeed one of the highest forms of creative power necessary for the survival of living forms, human individuals, and social organizations. The minimum of its mysterious grace is indispensable for physical, moral, and mental growth of human beings and societies. It is the noblest and best antidote against all forms of interhuman struggle and against criminal, morbid, and suicidal tendencies. It is the loftiest educational force and inspirer of creativity in all fields of human endeavor. Finally, it is the heart and soul of freedom and of all religious and moral values.

IV

As to the source of this love energy and the means for its production, accumulation, and application, we know that in potential form it is given to man as a part of his biological endowment as a "social animal." The magnitude of this potential seems to vary from man to man. The amount of this potential love, transformed into actual or "kinetic" energy, is largely conditioned by the kind of man-made culture in which the individual is found and by the kind of social interaction he has with others. The greater the biological endowment of love in the members of a given society, the more do individuals interact according to the rule, "love begets love," the more their social institutions and culture are permeated by the "climate of love," and the greater the output of love energy by the society as a whole.

This output can be notably increased by recourse to several efficient techniques for the production and accumulation of this energy. Despite our meager understanding of them, some thirty techniques are known to exist. With increased research our understanding of them may deepen and new ones may be invented. The known techniques range widely in complexity from the rudest to the most subtle. As examples of the simpler techniques can be mentioned the use of various chemical, physical, and biotic agents; training in posture and control of the autonomic nervous system; and techniques of conditioned reflexes, habit formation, mechanical drilling, and punishment and reward. More refined methods involve rational persuasion and scientific demonstration, reinforced by mobilization of man's emotional, affective, and volitional forces; use of the heroic examples; direct life experience; and the inspiration of the fine arts. The subtle techniques to increase the altruism of man include stimulation of man's creativity; concentration, meditation, and self-examination; and especially the complex methods of the Yogas, of Zen Buddhism, of the founders of religions of love, and of the great monastic orders.

These lines give an idea about the sources of love-energy and the meager "know-how" of techniques of its production and accumulation. In this article there is no room for a detailed discussion of these problems. It suffices to say that if a small portion of the money and effort now spent for war purposes—or even for more effective use of the sources of physical energy—were spent for research and cultivation of unselfish love, the beneficial results of such an endeavor would be most rewarding. If, in addition, every one of us would decrease in his personal life a portion of hateful emotions and actions of enmity and would increase that of emotions and actions of unselfish love—to all human beings—by this change of our mind and behavior we could improve the moral climate of mankind and could contribute to a lasting peace much more than by all the operations of power politics and armament race. The time has come when the intensive cultivation of the creative role has become everybody's business.

Part II

Metaphysical Aspects
of Love

The articles in this second part address the nature of the metaphysical climate that underlies the mutual attraction and union
between the sexes.

The milieu in which these relationships take place is a universal
one with metaphysical overtones. The world-view that emerges
is one of a background of unseen energies at many levels behind
the visible world, energies which we use and which affect all we
do. In this context, the ability of a human to feel and express love
is seen as deriving from a relation to a Universal love.

The concept that all human interactions are expressed with and
through a universal life force has been nurtured through the ages
and is expressed here once again. A theme that runs through the
following articles advises us that our energies can be volitionally
transformed to another level of consciousness. The same creative
power of the universe that provides us with life also gives us
sexual energy. This energy, the authors maintain, does not have
to be expressed only physically; it can be transmuted into other
channels, such as an active concern for others, self-realization,
and even self-transcendence. Self-transcending love rests on an
awareness of the higher, divine reaches of the universal energy
behind sex. The authors explore here some of the aspects of this
metaphysical view and through it how a self-transcending love
may be generated.

Part II

Metaphysical Aspects
of Love

9

We must learn human love before we can learn divine Love. If we put out the smaller lights of our human loves before the sun of divine Love dawns in our hearts, we do nothing but plunge ourselves into the darkness of a loveless life.
    I. K. Taimni, Glimpses into
    the Psychology of Yoga

An Interview with
RENÉE WEBER
by Scott Miners

Plato's Ladder of Love

(The interview format, so popular today, seems most appropriate to express Plato's views as it is an example of his own open-ended, informal style—the dialogue. Ed.)

We have all heard of Platonic love and assume it relates to Plato's philosophy. What exactly is it?

Platonic love is the most misunderstood of all of Plato's concepts. Through the years people, most of them unfortunately not knowing Plato nor having read him, have thought that Platonic love means ascetic or non-sexual love. This is not correct. In the *Symposium*, Plato tries to bring out that sexual love is a natural part of the scheme of things, but it has infinitely profound roots.

Is there then a cosmic principle of love in Platonic thought?

71

Yes, for Plato love *is* a cosmic principle. He sees love as a ladder consisting of seven steps which reach from the love of one person to a love of the highest realities in the universe. The whole of the *Symposium*, the most important dialogue that Plato has written on love, is devoted to love in its various aspects. He makes the point that, though I fall in love with one person, drawn by the beauty of that person, to remain exclusively fixed on that one person is to remain on the first step of a ladder which has many more rungs to it.

The entry to this ladder for most humans is through the physical love of one person. The immortality that one seeks is via this one person, in terms of procreation and so on, which Plato says is innate in the mortal human being. However, to remain fixed on this first step of the ladder of love is to remain undeveloped compared to all that a human being could grow into and develop. It is a regression. Plato is not otherworldly; he doesn't deny the body and the love of male and female. His point is that if I fail to widen this entry-level relationship and climb via the first step to the other six, I have remained in a regressive state. The further steps are not only possible but are the natural unfolding of the human condition.

Where else can love take us? How can the love of the male and female grow into wider dimensions?

The whole dialogue in the *Symposium* is Plato's answer to that question. The context of the dialogue is that of a number of speeches on the subject of love. In fact, the word *symposium* means "drinking together." Various figures in Athenian society are gathered together discussing the nature, the meaning, the implications of love. Those up to the time of Socrates' turn have given various descriptions of love, and all of them have been one-sided—though not false —descriptions. One person has said love makes us do noble deeds to be worthy of the beloved. Someone has said love is a kind of frenzy and madness, while others such as Aristophanes, have termed love a seeking of your other half in the world.

You might ask, "How did the other half get lost?" Plato has Aristophanes say that the human condition was such that all of us were double-figured and double-faced human beings. There were three sorts of humans in the world. In the man/man figure even in silhouette the whole body was composed of double-faced, double-bodied male figures. Another was composed of female, and finally there was the male/female.

Could you call this the androgyne?

This was the androgynous figure where one half was female and one half male. In this lovely fable and myth, designed to bring out a very profound point (as we will see later). Aristophanes says that all these double-figured beings transgressed against the gods, and as punishment the gods split them in half. So love looked at from that perspective is literally seeking your other half.

Cast into Platonic terms, this fable has far wider implications and will fit into Platonic metaphysics and ethics. Another way of saying that love is looking for your other half is to say that in our present state we are not complete and the stirrings of love are precisely this search for completion.

This is related to the ladder of love concept in the Symposium?

Yes. This search for completion is obvious on the first of the seven steps of the ladder of love when you fall passionately in love with one human being. This is natural as you seek to complete yourself. Then you beget, procreate in beauty, as Plato says. This is part of the idea of love. But you do not remain there. If your entire expression of love is restricted to that one person, and especially to the physical form of that one person, you have cut yourself off from the vast universe and from the vast potential in humanity.

Plato says that love "is a madness which is a divine gift and a source of the chiefest blessings granted to man."

Exactly. So he has a very exalted view of the love between the sexes, and in fact he does not want us to underestimate its scope and meaning. I think he uses the word *madness* to apply to this first level, or rung, on the ladder of love because under the influence of physical passion we often lose our perspective and our priorities. He describes how the soul is so eager for contact with the other person that it will lose its judgment. When you are very much in love, it is as if the universe is concentrated in that other person.

You have eyes only for that person.

You have eyes only for that person. This is not necessarily false. Later Plato says in a sense the universe *is* in that person. But you have to draw it out; you have to see not just that person but the universe in that person. In that early stage however, passionate love is almost like a madness.

The madness is only half of it, however, because it is a divine madness, and Plato never loses sight of that. It is something wondrous, mysterious, and far deeper and potentially more spiritual than human beings realize.

Is Plato speaking of a type of love at the first level of the ladder that is of the purest motivation, or is he speaking of the average love relation that has a good deal of selfish motivation attached to it?

That is a very good question and it is of central importance in understanding Plato's outlook on love. Everything he said in the *Symposium* about love—in loving the person you are loving the universe and vice versa—is said of unselfish, genuine love. This comes up again in the *Phaedrus,* which is also about love, physical and otherwise. In the *Phaedrus* Plato distinguishes very explicitly and overtly between these two types of love. As we will see later, the physical relationship merely as the means for pleasure, Plato does not support.

Would Plato say then that the sexual relationship is more

than an instinctual drive because it can serve to set a person on the path to self-transcending love?

Yes, with the caveat that you brought up earlier, provided that this is a genuine, loving, and selfless passion. If it is merely a use of the other for my own selfish gratification then, in virtually all the Platonic dialogues, he dissociates himself from it. It is a pitfall and danger. It is not love and will not lead anywhere except to blindness and to craving (this latter point he shares with Buddhism). Plato is often accused of being ascetic, otherworldly, disapproving of the body, and, while there is some truth to that, we have to be careful not to overstate that position. The *Symposium* and the *Phaedrus* provide the correctives to the mainly ascetic tone of the other Platonic dialogues.

Platonic love, then, is precisely a love that is so wide, so stirring, and so universal that, though it begins with a love of the beautiful form, it ends with a love of the form of Beauty itself, an eternal principle of the universe. Therefore as you develop and understand the deeper implications of the Platonic meaning of love, you are led in a most natural way (though through the catalyst of the one beautiful form) to a realization that all beautiful forms are lovable. You generalize and become sensitive to all beautiful forms.

Constantly he uses the word *beauty*. Whether physically embodied or not, Beauty in ideas becomes as real, and in fact more real than physical beauty.

When he uses the word beauty and universalizes the concept or archetype of Beauty itself as it manifests in form, does he connect it with love?

Love and beauty are connected. You see beauty when you are in love. As you progress, you see in all beautiful forms the kind of beauty, feel the sort of exaltation, that you experienced when you first fell in love. As you grow and unfold under the notion of Platonic love, ever allowing love to pull you onward or upward, you have departed from the particular toward the many. But you are not yet at the universal.

You next see that the beauty of mind is, not only equally wondrous as beauty of form, but in fact more so. Plato says in the *Symposium* that even if a person's form is not so comely visually and physically, you fall in love with the quality of his or her mind. This is a progression from the concrete and the physical to the nonphysical, the non-material. From here under the influence and inspiration of love you move upward toward something yet more universal, more abstract.

That is Step 2?

No. Step 2 is loving all beautiful physical forms. Step 3 is loving beauty of mind regardless of the physical form it is associated with.

I see. Then what is the next step?

The fourth step of the ladder of love is the love of beautiful practices—ethics.

Putting away the dishes?

Yes, putting away the dishes. Fairness, justice, kindness, consideration—those too have beauty and can impel you to love. It is broader and more universal and leads to Step 5, which is a love of beautiful institutions. For example, the love of the way society works, when its institutions are conceived with balance and harmony, therefore in beauty. It isn't just a concern with the family. It is a love of government, culture, all the things that Plato cites in the *Republic* as instances of beautiful institutions. The philosopher who is a lover of wisdom falls in love with that kind of harmony, where the good of the whole is the primary concern and not the good only of the isolated individual, the family unit, or even the little community. Plato is concerned with a holistic society, with the whole. This is the fifth step.

From here the soul soars (a word he uses in the *Phaedrus*) to the sixth step on the ladder of love. In the *Symposium* the sixth manifestation of the growth of love is a gigantic leap upward toward the universal and the abstract, and this

Plato calls "science," i.e., knowledge and understanding. On the sixth step you are in love with beautiful science, which now articulates, not just the laws governing the individual or the family or even the society as a whole, but something that transcends the local environment. The beauty of science is something that is universal, such as the Pythagorean theorem.

Or the biology of the Earth?

Exactly. All of that. Or the Einstein universe, which ultimately includes the whole cosmos. Plato obviously did not know much detail about science, but he intuited the essence of what science could be like. It reveals beauty, harmony, and order, a position which discloses his Pythagorean roots. You can fall in love with that as deeply as you can with a man or a woman. The great scientists, such as Einstein, Kepler, Galileo, Newton, said that in articulating the laws of the universe they were studying the logic and order and beauty of the mind of God. Many of them were Platonists. Giordano Bruno, 16th century philosopher and cosmologist, allowed himself to be burned at the stake rather than deny his beautiful scientific insight or vision of an infinitive and interconnected universe. All that is part of what Plato means when he speaks of the love of science, *scientia*, knowledge.

He sees human beings as an integral part of this overall cosmic design or beauty?

It is the human being who has articulated these laws and so brought them into palpable form for us, and it is the human being who falls in love with them. In the case of Giordano Bruno, who was executed by the Inquisition in the year 1600, you could say it was a kind of falling in love with the laws of the universe to so deep a degree that, just as a man will defend the woman he loves against an aggressor, so Bruno defended his vision of the infinite universe against attack and chose death rather than deny that love. This is genuine love. Einstein, too, had the love of the mysterious and of the beauty in the universe.

Now Socrates makes a speech about Step 7 which is the highlight of the dialogue. You know that something sacred and important is about to be said when Socrates begins to speak at this stage of the *Symposium*. He claims thai everything he is about to say he learned from a sacred priestess by the name of Diotima. Here Plato is preparing the audience to expect something important and weighty, and indeed we are not disappointed.

Diotima says there are the lesser mysteries of love and the greater mysteries of love. In her revelation to Socrates long ago she described the seven steps on the ladder. The lesser mysteries are composed of steps one, as discussed earlier, and steps two, three, and four. But as she explains how we go up the ladder from these to the greater mysteries of love, she pauses. There is a kind of solemn moment in the speech of Socrates. She says to Socrates, "I don't know if you will be able to follow this." Whenever Plato has a character say this, you know, through internal evidence reconstructed from other dialogues, that he is about to articulate an esoteric teaching. This is surrounded by great solemnity, a kind of pause that scholars have noted. He advertises it, as if proclaiming that something important is about to be said.

The greater mysteries of love (Steps 5, 6 and 7) evolve around the vision of the universal. The most important moment in Diotima's speech in the *Symposium* is when she says that between steps six and seven we have changed almost imperceptibly from mundane realities to the highest realities in the universe. Plato uses the word *suddenly*. He says that after going through all these steps, when we come to step seven there is a difference in kind, although it is also a difference in degree. *Suddenly* you see not the manifestation or an example of beauty, but Beauty itself. That is Step 7 on the ladder of love. It is its epitome, the high point of the sacred mysteries, as Diotima calls them. Love here expresses itself as the love of the everlasting manifestation of Beauty itself. In other words, you fall in love not just with a form of beauty but with its essence, which makes all things beautiful. This is Beauty at its source.

Diotima makes a memorable speech, as the following extract from the *Symposium* shows:

> This, my dear Socrates, is that life above all others which man should live, in the contemplation of Beauty absolute; a Beauty which if you once beheld, you would see not to be after the measure of gold, and garments, fair boys and youths, whose presence now entrances you; and you and many a one would be content to live seeing them only and conversing with them without meat or drink, if that were possible—you only want to look at them and to be with them. But what if the man had eyes to see the true Beauty—the divine Beauty, I mean, pure and clear and unalloyed, not clogged with the pollutions of mortality and all the colors and vanities of human life—thither looking, and holding converse with the true Beauty simple and divine? Remember how in that communion only, beholding beauty with the eye of the mind, he will be enabled to bring forth, not images of beauty, but realities (for he has hold not of an image but of a reality), and bringing forth and nourishing true virtue to become the friend of God and be immortal, if mortal man may. Would that be an ignoble life?

This sounds like a visionary contact with a supreme reality, or truth.

This *is* a kind of vision. It is like seeing the sun in the allegory of the Cave in the *Republic*. After living with your back to it and seeing only shadows on the wall, you suddenly see it! It is fusion with the beloved form, completeness. In a deeper sense, this evokes what Aristophanes described; the lover seeks completeness, not just through the other half with which he was originally united, but completeness by union with the eternal and nonmaterial form itself. That is a kind of immortality.

Secular and personal love was the beginning of this search for wholeness. The end point is to have a vision of what underlies the universe and what makes it go round. Therefore, falling in love on the seventh step of the ladder of love is union with the source of being. It unites the individual with his ultimate, infinite source. It is a kind of mystical doctrine of love, and that is Platonic love. It is a stirring and inspiring view that far transcends the notion of just holding hands with another.

This usually starts between a man and woman and the attraction between the two sets the stage for the perception of beauty of love?

Exactly. That is what is so wonderful. This shows us that people underestimate Platonic love. It does not devalue the love between a man and a woman—it shows rather that they are part of this upward pull toward the divine, the spiritual and immortal. Physical love is one such catalyst which leads to falling in love with the whole universe. We start by falling in love with one person, in fact, with his or her physical beauty. We become increasingly aware of other dimensions until finally, in loving the essence or eternal form of Beauty, we have fallen in love with the whole universe. It is a cosmic love that works back and forth between the particular and the universal. It begins and interacts with the singular daily physical aspect of life.

The climax of this speech by Diotima is so important that I feel that I should quote from the *Symposium* again. Diotima says: "He who has been instructed thus far in the things of love, and who has learned to see the beautiful in due order and succession when he comes towards the end will suddenly perceive a nature of wondrous beauty, and this, Socrates, is the final cause of all our former toils." In other words, this is the moment to which all the other steps up the ladder of love have led in a fully developed and mature human being.

What is it that we fall in love with? Plato says we perceive beauty in its timeless aspect: "—a nature which in the first place is everlasting, not growing and decaying, or waxing and waning"; secondly, not relativistic, "not fair in one point of view and foul in another or at one time or in one relation or at one place fair, at another time or in another relation or at another place foul." But what is it? It is "Beauty absolute, separate, simple, and everlasting, which without diminution and without increase, or any change, is imparted to the ever-growing and perishing beauties of all other things." Diotima concludes: "This, my dear Socrates . . . is that life above all others which man should live, in the contemplation of Beauty absolute."

Plato would say then that love is at the core of, or is an aspect of universal life?

Yes. In the *Phaedrus*, Plato uses another metaphor to bring out the same idea of love as mediating between the mortal and immortal, between the specific and the universal, between the concrete and the abstract. In the *Phaedrus* the lovers, because of their love, are impelled to seek higher regions, purer forms. So they sprout wings. The wings enable them to soar to the rim of the universe where they see the eternal forms, i.e., the essence of temporal things. Even the most passionate physical lovers will receive their wings by means of their love if it is pure, and on these wings they will rise upward and glimpse the timeless dimensions of being.

Then Plato brings in another metaphor, that of a chariot pulled by two horses, one white and one black. The black steed represents impure or selfish love, where one uses the other person only for physical gratification or pleasure. A person ruled by the black horse clamors for immediate gratification and is always selfishly oriented. If this dark, ignoble steed rules, he upsets the balance of the team of horses. This type of love cannot lead to the universal because its selfish and intemperate style makes that impossible. This brings out Plato's ascetic streak. He cautions against this kind of love because it is excessive, imbalanced, self-centered. It isn't love at all; it is self-love. But if the lover really loves, the white horse helps to rule so that the whole team—the white horse, the black horse, and the charioteer—can move upward toward the "rim of heaven" and there behold the eternal truths. The white horse balances us by its reason, wholeness, altruism, and concern for the other.

The black steed then is a symbol for the physical senses, whereas the white horse is that which is beyond the senses?

That, generally, is the idea.

Then, who, or what, does the driver of the team symbolize?

The driver of the team symbolizes the soul and the vision of the soul—reason, purity, spiritual longing. Love can be the very carriage, the vehicle, to lead us to another dimension of being, and to provide glimpses of other states of consciousness in the very act of love.

In modern times we could say Plato holds that in a very deep and profound sexual union there is a foretaste of the ecstasy of the union with the divine spiritual reality that underlies the universe. It is a poor man's immortality. It is a small manifestation of divine union, and yet human beings certainly value sexual and love experience. Through a deep sexual love, each of us tastes self-transcendence and self-forgetfulness for brief moments of time.

At step seven on the ladder, that self-transcendence which was brief and momentary becomes the natural state where we dwell all the time. The self has disappeared into the background; in the foreground there shine the eternal verities, the good, the true, the beautiful, perceived as undiluted and transparent to the soul capable of seeing them. Thus love has enabled us from the beauties of the earth to mount upward toward heaven, as Plato says. What began in time ends in eternity; what began with the touch of one person ends in the embrace of the universe.

10

Knowing of the Male,
  But staying with the Female,
    One becomes the humble Valley of the World.
Being the Valley of the World
  He never deviates from his real nature
  And thus returns to the innocence of the infant.
                                    Lao-tse, Tao te Ching

CLAUDE BRAGDON

The Worship of Eros

Anyone attempting to deal with the problems of present-day life other than superficially cannot avoid a discussion of love, but he will approach the subject with trepidation. For love, that pure spring, reflecting heaven, appears to have become a sort of cesspool, now stirred to its nethermost depths of stench. It would be happier to pass, clamping the nose and blinking the eye, but that is impossible.

The initial difficulty is one of definition: what does one mean by the word "love"? Is the subject to be treated biologically or theologically—as personal passion or as impersonal compassion? Is love sex-hunger or soul-fulfillment? Or is it the adoration of the Most High?

Love is perhaps all of these, and there may be a synthesis which reconciles them; but let us begin by thinking of love simply as an emotion which creates, transforms, organizes,

and destroys with an energy transcending any other emotion. We may not know what love is, but we may know what
it is not, for if love lacks this dynamic, dithyrambic quality
it is not love.

The passion assumes many forms and takes many directions—often at right angles to one another—but its supreme
human expression is in the love of man for woman and of
woman for man. Pre-adolescent and homosexual loves are
not as abnormal nor as uncommon as we used to think
them, but it is only when fully nubile and bipolar that the
Beautiful Monster develops teeth and claws and unfurls
empyrean-storming wings. For the sex-instinct and the
spiritual nature awaken together and are strangely inter-
mingled, sometimes scarcely distinguishable, religious
ecstasy and sheer eroticism intoxicating the consciousness
at the same time and in a similar way. This is a mystery
the meaning of which evades us, but its importance cannot
be gainsaid, for it negates all those current materialistic
conceptions of love as solely a biological necessity, scarcely different from nutrition and excretion. At such a theory
of love it is not necessary even to glance.

The polar opposite of this is the Oriental idea of love as
set forth in the *Upanishads*. This, though deeply mystical,
possesses the advantage that it reconciles all contradictions
and fits all facts. What it amounts to, briefly, is that all
loves are of the self for the Self. If this statement is too
condensed and cryptic it might be elaborated in the
language of latter-day psychology something after this
fashion:

Behind the phenomena of consciousness, both objective
and subjective—even behind consciousness itself—there is
some ultimate reality or being of which the physically conditioned consciousness is only a reflection or representa-
tion. This inscrutable "being" is therefore called the Unconscious, not because it is so, but because we are in the
main unconscious of it. On the contrary, it is an organizing
and intelligent principle which emerges in clearness and
power in proportion as the organic functions with which

the consciousness of waking life is associated cease their activity. The two are divided by what is called "the psychophysical threshold of sensibility," and this is a movable threshold, the conscious capturing and making its own ever more and more of the Unconscious, the Unconscious pouring ever more and more of itself into the slender but unfillable cup of the personal consciousness. This process and this relation constitute the only and all-inclusive "love-affair," which is between self-existence and self-realization —the Self and the self.

With the aid of this explanation the reader is now better prepared to understand the statement that all loves are of the self for the Self. It is a logical necessity inherent in the nature of monism. The whole of Oriental philosophy is summed up in three words: "Thou are That"—thy soul is Brahman. The meaning and purpose of life is to bring about increasingly this realization, to become *that which thou art.* Love, of every kind and degree, is the effective and ordained approach to this transcendence, by reason of its *transforming power.* For love, be it that of the craftsman for his work, the religionist for his god, or the lover for his mistress, liberates into a greater largeness, pushes forward into the Unconscious the psycho-physical threshold. Each party to a love-relation becomes thus for the other a pathway to liberation, or, what is the same thing, a means of greater self-realization. However little lovers may be conscious of it, they desire one another in order that they may become *That.* It is on this account they find one another sweet, for "This Self is the honey of all beings, and all beings are the honey of this Self."

That all loves are of the self for the Self is reiterated almost to weariness in the sacred books of the East: "Therefore if you like, Lady, I will explain it to thee, and mark well what I say: Verily a husband is not dear that you may love a husband, but that you may love the Self, therefore a husband is dear." And this formula is repeated over and over to similar effect: wife, sons, wealth, cattle, worlds, Devas, Vedas—everything, in fact, is not dear in order that you may love everything, but that you may love the Self.

Now, all this may seem vague, mystical, and even a little childish to those unaccustomed to Eastern modes of thought, and unable to interpret them in terms of Western ways of thinking, or of their own experience, but here we have an idea of the utmost importance at the present time: that love is the path to man's lost paradise. By coming to understand love in this new way, and on that understanding establishing a new kind of relation, lovers may attain to liberation not only from their own narrower selves, but from the narrower selves of one another, which is ever the unhealed wound in Adonis' side. Recognizing that the love of persons is in its very nature limited and has its term in time, each serves and worships the Self as incarnate in the other—that aspect of the Self of which each is as it were the opposite, the man loving and coming to know the Eternal Feminine through and by means of that ephemeral and temporal aspect of Her which is the personal woman; and she loving and paying homage to the Eternal Masculine through and by means of His embodiment in the man of her choice. In such a condition of mind and spirit, free from shame, pride, vanity, lustfulness, fear, and everything else that might muddy the waters of the sacred fount, the "body's lord" of each is enabled to contact its own Immortal Lover. The pair become points of contact and vehicles of communication of their own higher selves, one with the Great Self, charged with divine, immortal life—"of dateless brood of Heaven and Eternity."

Of course what we observe all about us is the direct antithesis of this: men and women tormenting and coercing one another, poisoning and draining one another's sacred fount (as it can be drained and poisoned if its place of replenishment is dammed), practicing duplicities, plotting betrayals, perpetrating sub-human—nay, sub-animal— crimes, and all in the name of love. As Ouspensky says, "In the majority of cases love, as it exists in modern life, has become a trifling-away of feelings and sensations. It is difficult, in the conditions which govern life in the world, to imagine a love which will not interfere with mystical aspirations. Temples of love and the mystical celebration of love's mysteries exist no longer." In the same essay, however, he strikes a more hopeful note: "Love is the eternally burning fire in which humanity and all the world are being incessantly purified, all the forces of the human spirit and of genius are being evolved and refined; and perhaps, indeed, from this same fire or by its aid a new force will arise which shall deliver from the chains of matter all who follow where it leads."

Now, just because love can be such a devastating force in life, the source of emotional and physical miseries without number, it may be also the most powerful of all agents of regeneration, a veritable fountain of new life; for everywhere action is equal to reaction, and the depth of a shadow is an index of the brilliance of a light—"fire will freeze and frost will burn." The Master said: "In all ways the sons of man follow My way," and of all ways "the follower of union" is deemed the highest—"higher than men of penance, higher than men of learning; the follower of union is higher than men of works." Now, the lover is preeminently "the follower of union," for the aim of love *is* union; but if lovers desire only union with one another *as persons*, that love is exhausted in fulfillment, satiety and boredom supervene, or "hatred's swift repulsions play." If on the other hand they desire union with the divine through and by means of one another, instead of being like easily broken and quickly emptied bottles they become conductors from an inexhaustible reservoir of life.

Upon this conception of love is evidently founded the Oriental cult of *Sahaja*, the aim of which appears to be spiritual freedom (*moksha*) through and by means of a certain attitude and relation possible to be established between lovers. Sahaja is *love as a means of initiation*—an escape, not *from* life, but *into* life. Ananda Coomaraswamy, the distinguished Oriental scholar, has this to say on the subject:

> In India we could not escape the conviction that sexual love has a deep and spiritual significance. There

is nothing with which we can better compare the 'mystic union' of the finite with its infinite ambient—that one experience which proves itself and is the only ground of faith—than the self-oblivion of earthly lovers locked in each other's arms where 'each is both.' Physical proximity, contact, and interpenetration are the expressions of love only because love is the recognition of identity. These two are one flesh because they have remembered their unity of spirit. This is moreover a fuller identity than the mere sympathy of two individuals; and each as individual has now no more significance for the other than the gates of heaven for one who stands within. It is like an algebraic equation where the equation is the only truth, and the terms may stand for anything. The least intrusion of the ego, however, involves a return to the illusion of duality.

While it is true that all true lovers, simply by reason of their being such, are candidates for this initiation, only a small number possess the qualifications necessary for success, nor are these often able to command the right conditions. For it is imperative that both belong to the same dimension, inhabit, that is, the same circle of consciousness, be peers of one another, karmically related, molded of the same moral paste. "Cosmic" love is so strange and paradoxical a thing that to the "base-born and passion-torn" who only

> Whine, and flatter and regret,
> And kiss, and couple and beget,

it is not recognizable as love at all. Not only are they incapable of realizing it, but they are incapable even of conceiving of it: the plenum cannot but appear to them a vacuum, for the same reason that to the materialist Nirvana is nothingness.

For such love is possible of attainment only when nothing personal remains: it is without desire, for he who desires is still athirst; it is equally without fear, because "fear arises from a second only." The cosmic lover has surrendered his will in order to be free from willing; he requires nothing, and offers nothing to the beloved, acknowledging a perfection which cannot be added to:

> They give and take no pledge or oath,
> Nature is the bond of both.
> No prayer persuades, no flattery fawns,
> Their noble meanings are their pawns.

They are not attracted by pleasure or repelled by pain; although they play with the most dangerous passions, they are ever the bow and never the arrow. "*Sahaja*," says Coomaraswamy, "has nothing to do with the cult of pleasure. It is the doctrine of the Tao, the path of non-pursuit. All that is best for us comes of itself into our hands —but if we strive to overtake it, it perpetually eludes us." These lovers deny one another nothing, yet never fall; they drink deep beyond the point of drunkenness and achieve only clarity and sobriety. This love is not a means to an end, because it is at once a means and an end. It cannot therefore be associated with social and eugenic ideas: the longing for children is a longing for possessions, and the longing for possessions is a longing for the world. Neither can it be associated with ideas of contraception, having their root in the feeling of fear, because "perfect love casteth out fear." "Forbearance" and "self-sacrifice" do not enter into this relation: founded on utter freedom and familiarity, it brings an unsought, unshaken serenity in moments of greatest intimacy by reason of the absence of all taboos and the presence of Presence—the fire on the altar, the god in the sanctuary, the entire nature attuned to the worship of the Most High. Here is nothing done for oneself or for one another, no effort made to evoke response, none to withhold it. This love has nothing to do with passion and surrender: it knows no sin, no shame, no despair, no exultation, for it is "the peace that passeth all understanding," and these things mean no more to it than waves mean to the unfathomed depths of the sea.

11

They are free, yes, but liberated, no. Free to make
love, but not free of the pressures of the inherited
habits, of current customs and fashions, and of
personal environmental demands upon the sexual
desires.

Jacques Mousseau, L'amour a refaire

DANE RUDHYAR

The Procreative, Recreative, Transformative and Social Aspects of Sex

Hardly any topic occupies the attention of human beings
more insistently than sex, except perhaps money. Effective
sexual activity is deeply felt as a manifestation of biopsychological power; and the capacity to make and spend
money is identified as the most basic form of social power.
The power drive is indeed strong in human beings, particularly, but certainly not exclusively, in males.

Biologically speaking, the development of male and
female sexual polarities, whenever it first occurred in the
biosphere, had for its purpose the production of immense
possibilities of variations in the genetic theme of Man.
The asexual type of organism simply reproduces itself
ad infinitum, whether it be through simple division of one
whole into two exactly similar ones (*mitosis*) or in some
other more complex process. Sexualization leads to a

variety of genetic combinations. It also produces a host of problems of relationship, for duality compels the two separate factors to seek ways of recombining. The recombination of differentiated organisms is a process in which the possibility of inadequacy in the coming together is a source of potential conflict. Conflict is inherent in the biosphere, whose basic law seems to be "eat or be eaten"— also called by ancient Indian writers "the law of the fish" (big fish eating little fish). But with sex, another kind of conflict is introduced: conflict based on the unfitness of the recombining units. Either the two, or one of them, are not totally ready for the combination when an urge for it— naturally or artificially stimulated—comes, or the shapes and characters of the two do not exactly match, physiologically, or even more in human beings, psychologically.

The potentiality of conflict, and in psychologically evolved persons, of misunderstandings and resentment— leading in many cases to the development of a sense of failure, guilt or impotency—cannot be avoided, for it is inherent in all dualisms; it can, however, be greatly lessened if sexual activity is not given only one basic meaning, but instead is understood to have several aspects and to meet several easily differentiated purposes. In other words, sex is not just sex—a need to be satisfied for only one purpose. The sexual drive in human beings operates at different levels, and four levels are particularly noticeable and significant. If one person, consciously or semi-consciously, seeks in sex the fulfillment of a need at one of these levels, but his or her partner expects sexual contacts to have meaning and fill a need at another level, frustration and resentment, if not overt conflict, are inevitable. To ascertain, before the action begins, what the other person expects of it is the wise approach to "making love;" it is even more wise to become involved in a relationship meant to have at least a degree of permanency and to lead to joint fulfillment and happiness.

What then are these four main levels at which sexual relationships operate in our modern societies?

The first and basic level is evidently the biological. Biological sex is a reproductive method by which life-species insure their perpetuation, generation after generation. It is instinctual, and all instincts are compulsive: Plants and animals have no possibility of suppressing or deliberately modifying their operation. Human beings, however, are able to partially and even, in rarer cases, totally control the sexual impulses. The result of such control is to transfer the instinctual energy, and the psychic yearnings which accompany its arousal, to the level of inner feelings and mental imagery.* The transferred urge normally seeks new forms of satisfaction, and these may be personal or social; they may also be of immensely varied types. But they may also be frustrated by cultural, moral or social imperatives and taboos. The result is the formation of psychological complexes, which we may symbolically define as whirlpools of psychic energy unable to be resolved into the mainstream of vitality. Other results may be crystallizations of fear, an anxiety or impotent revolt blocking the natural, rhythmic circulation of the libido.

Biological sex is fundamentally an unconscious, non-deliberate power. The organism-as-a-whole is "possessed" by it; and whatever consciousness exists in the organism is fascinated by the nearly irresistible glamor with which life surrounds and pervades sexual fulfillment. Yet resistance is possible, and definite lines of resistance are quite rigidly set down in the name of social morality, or even (in the case

---

*When I use the term psychic, I refer to what I consider the overtones of fundamental drives and changes occurring at the level of biological functions and impulses. Biological pressures and activities induce parallel, or at least definitely related changes in that part of the total personality I define as the psychic realm. It is a realm not only of "feelings," but of mental images. Psychic imagery can be induced by several sources, but the main one today has to do directly or indirectly with what occurs at the biological level where *all* instincts, not only sexual ones, operate. Abnormal genetic factors may thus strongly affect the feelings, the emotions and the mental imagery emerging, often autonomously and uncontrollably, into the part of the mind that is a servant of biological instinct and a reflector for organic changes, agreeable, painful or traumatic as they may be.

of incest) of concern over the genetic inheritance of potential progeny. The biological purpose of sex is, of course, the bearing of children, and this purpose in human beings often takes the form of an emotional yearning for children, particularly in the mother-to-be. But as human beings live in the state of society and are constantly subjected to the power of social and religious values and expected forms of behavior (second level), the instinctual yearning is made to fit into the collective patterns (including mere fashion) which at least channel its conscious manifestations—or rather the manifestations acceptable to an ego, whose nature is to establish set patterns of adjustment between social-cultural imperatives and the satisfaction of biological needs.

In healthy human beings living in societies that generally allow the power of instinct to fulfill the purpose strictly defined by its release in answer to basic human needs, biological sex rather easily finds its satisfaction, and of itself should entail no situations of conflicts. The female's resistance and play of escape is part of the working out of the problems of overcoming any difference in individual character in the aroused partners. But when human beings become increasingly individualized and social or moral obstacles interfere with the fulfillment of sexual relationships, all sorts of problems arise. These obstacles in fact become means whereby the urge to become individualized in revolt against social-cultural interferences gains strength —often a tragic kind of strength.

The more a person becomes distinctly, perhaps violently, individualized (third level), the more he or she experiences a poignant feeling of separateness—then isolation and perhaps total alienation from the social scene and even from other human beings. These feelings of separateness and isolation are nevertheless challenged by the instinctual drive for biological union with another sexually complementary human being. The result is either deepening psychoneurosis or sexual situations in which the elements of conflict, abnormality, and perhaps violence blended with despair are present in a more or less destructive form, which at the very least inhibits happiness in relationship and often produces a tragic sense of impotency.

Sex, then, most often becomes devaluated into a rather meaningless function, a play to soothe the pressure of frustrated biological impulses, and perhaps a way to exert power over another human being. Sex may also be deliberately used not only to counteract the loneliness of the single person, but to attempt also to reach a level of consciousness and power which, one feels, can only come from the interaction—even if it means the clash—of two polarized bodies and their nervous systems.

In the first instance, sex as a play (which one hopes will have no biological consequences) is enjoyed as a kind of escape from boredom, weariness or tension; it tends to become refined, cultured, and used as a search for unusual and if possible always new sensations. If both partners operate at the same level, and find in sexual play pleasure, excitement and a temporary heightened feeling of "being-in-the-body"—an antidote against intellectual, professional or business weariness and emptiness—all may be well, provided pregnancy does not result. Unfortunately, one of the partners may operate at the biological level out of which deep emotions and a longing for permanency and progeny normally arise, while the other sees sex only as a play and an escape—or even perhaps as a way to enjoy a sense of power over his or her partner. Then the interpersonal situation may create acute tension and unhappiness in the deeply involved partner, while the recreative intention of the other is also frustrated, perhaps by emotional scenes.

Sex can be used at another (fourth) level as a transformative and regenerative process; in some cases, and particularly in some cultures, as a ritual in which the man and woman consciously experience the rhythmic action of the impersonal power of life in its bipolar manifestation as this power moves their bodies and sets their consciousness afire. Today, because of the relative popularity of India's tantra philosophy, we are hearing a great deal about such experiences, or rather in most cases their sentimentalized reflections. To these are added for good measure the romantic concept of "soul-mates." What is involved, exceptions notwithstanding, is an emotional attempt to escape from, or at least seek an alternative to the type of egocentric, intellectual existence so prevalent in our present society. A poignant dissatisfaction with the superficial concerns, the narrow horizons and the insistent demands of what they call their "self" impels and at times compels an increasing number of people to long for a kind of dissolution into some vast, transcendent state of being, some ecstatic mode of consciousness and feeling. Sexual fulfillment seems to many the only way open to them. Even the tensions and dramatic scenes so frequent in a man-woman relationship can be forgotten, but usually not resolved insofar as their causes are concerned, when the electrical energy of the sexual function explodes, annihilating for a time the gnawing feeling of ego-insecurity and isolation. The feeling-experience may last only a brief moment, but so do most quasi-mystical "peak experiences." Nevertheless, the memory of such an impersonal state, which most people want to believe as being superpersonal, can remain: a subjective place of refuge when the dreariness of empty hours becomes too unbearable.

Thus sex only too often can be sought as an escape which, through a process of rationalization, the mind, filled with various hidden ideas, transforms and glorifies as sublimation. Yet any shadow is a witness to the reality of light. The raw and unconscious energy of life, when perfectly controlled by a will, disciplined by some age-old, more or less secret training can be heated up to a transmuting state in which a mysterious alchemy of consciousness and the repolarization of the whole being are possible. The key factor, however, is *control*; and control implies discipline. What is at stake is not an impetuous, emotional arousal, but a process whose phases should be understood, and whose results have to be accepted without reservation by the central "I," and not merely assented to by the glamorized mind.

Various symbols have been traditionally associated with this process of alchemical transmutation, not only of the sex-force but of the total biopsychic energy, much of which remains latent in the organism. The phoenix symbol and that of the serpent transformed into an eagle are well-known. Astrology relates them to the zodiacal sign Scorpio, which is so often associated with sexual activity *per se*. Such an association is only partially correct, for strictly biological, procreative sex should instead be related to the vernal sign Taurus, the symbol of fertility—but of unconscious, instinctual and compulsive sexual procreation. If Scorpio, an autumnal sign through which the Sun passes as the energies of vegetable life are withdrawing to the roots, is to be identified with sex, it should be clear that the identification is only with the *human* aspect of sex—sex, not as an *action* leading to more life, but as a *reaction* from a condition of self-individualization and isolation which calls for a determined effort to experience a complementary type of activity and consciousness.

This is why, at the human level of existence, sex, and the passionate, uncontrollable emotion of love which arises from the feeling that another person is just the one with whom the perfect union is possible, have so often an inherently tragic character—thus the association of great love with death. Such a love is a compulsive attempt to transcend what, in the present state of social and ego-centric existence, we are taught since childhood to accept as "living." The real transmutation process mentioned above can never be compulsive. It can be achieved only in clear consciousness and through intense self-discipline. It does not imply self-loss in an oceanic feeling, but rather the condensation of the ocean onto a perfectly formed chalice jointly built to receive the elixir of a transcendent power that is light rather than life.

I could end this meditation on sex here, but it seems best to return to the mundane realities associated with the power sex yields, today perhaps more than ever, in the social life of human beings whose main preoccupation is to rise to the top levels of the social order. Because of this preoccupation, sex becomes directly or indirectly associated with money. It becomes a form of social power and is used, personally or in business, to gain financial reward.

Social sex is everywhere today in American society. I am not speaking only of what, under its many forms—crude or subtle—we call prostitution. For example, being photographed in seductive postures with or without clothing can certainly be considered a form of prostitution, and there are many even more subtle and socially most acceptable forms. I am speaking also of the consistent use of sexual incentives in business and particularly in advertising. Such a practice can certainly be called a form of collective self-indulgence, which is far more pervasive and dangerous than personal self-indulgence. One might well speak of collective mental masturbation, or at least of an endless erogenous social play whose stakes are money. It would be quite legitimate to call this intellectual prostitution; it uses the power of imagination—one of the most important and characteristically human powers—and places it at the service of social incentives, just as the sex-haunted playboy uses the basic biological power of sex to fill a spiritually empty existence, or to soothe the semi-conscious pain of loneliness.

A human community—and in general any culture—has to have some kind of integrative power and a collective sense of value. In the past, this power and the value implied in its use came primarily through religion—in the broadest sense of the word. Today, especially in the U.S., the integrative power is that generated by the complex rituals of business and money-making. The collective goal is to acquire wealth, or at least the outward signs of prosperity. In a personal sense, the main drive is the drive for pleasure, and in it sex is made to play a considerable role. A loose kind of social ritual is involved; every class of people performing it in a particular and self-defining manner, modified only in part by individual preferences.

The individual person, though conditioned by his or her class and biopsychological temperament, theoretically need not participate in the ritual, but its pervasive influence is not easily dismissed, even in sexual matters which are also subject to collective fashions, especially at this time, during the chaotic transition-period in which mankind has to operate. The main issue, as I stated at the beginning, is for the persons meeting in terms of sexual activity, or of quasi-sexual and emotional experiences to be conscious of the level at which they are ready, willing and able to operate—and not only to be aware of, but honest (with themselves as well as with the other person) about their feelings and their expectations.

At every level many difficulties and obstacles or impediments of which the sexual partners may not be aware are inherent in sexual meetings. Wherever opposite polarities reach toward either an explosive burst of energy or the establishment of a steady current of useable power, problems of adjustment are bound to arise. They may be over· come in a dramatic crumbling of inhibitions or in a patient, and steadier, process of mutual give-and-take. Duality implies conflict. Wherever duality is stressed—and it is stressed in human personalities when each partner insists on acting as an "individual" with self-conscious rights—"harmony *through* conflicts" is the motto characterizing the situation.

The matter becomes increasingly complex when the psychological (or biopsychic) form taken by the ego-consciousness in its development through childhood and adolescence exhibits characteristics which are not in tune with the innate biological nature. There may be several reasons for the discordant personal situation which recently has taken an almost obsessive character in our country, becoming a collective and much-publicized issue. The development of a minority subculture based on homosexual behavior, male or female, in combination with the women's liberation movement, is now adding a new dimension to the collective and social aspect of the problems inherent in sexuality.

At the root of the situation is the evolutionary drive which is slowly, step by step, impelling an ever increasing number of human beings to strive after the development of consciousness at an intellectual level transcending not only the biological, but also the devotional; in other words, to become autonomous, unique, self-motivated, self-actualizing and (I might say) dis-collectivized individuals. This evolutionary process of individualization is worldwide. It affects a minority of human beings of both sexes in a focalized and transformative manner; and, directly or indirectly, through the pervasive, ubiquitous influence of the media and literature, a majority of the other people catch strong enough reflections of the process to experience an ambivalent reaction concerning both their biological instincts and the traditional religio-social taboos which had been stamped upon their developing egos.

The outcome is a generalized state of biopsychic and mental disassociation. It often manifests as unconscious hypocrisy or mild schizophrenia. Sexual activity, as a result, is hardly ever free from neurotic elements, either before, during or after the performance of sexual acts. We cannot, as individuals, change the collective situation or the massive impact of sex-haunted media and advertising. We can only try to become as clearly aware as we can of what impels us to act and react the way we do in pre-sexual, sexual or quasi-sexual meetings. We can only take nothing for granted, especially the value of publicized attitudes and fashionable behavior, and try to meet the other person as an individual, in clear, objective awareness of the level at which our own individual approach and main concerns in the situation are focused. We can only try to be, to the limit of our ability and readiness, intellectually as well as emotionally honest—even if it hurts.

12

*When the heart is flooded with love there is no room
in it for fear, for doubt, for hesitation. And it is this
lack of fear that makes for the dance. When each
partner loves so completely that he has forgotten to
ask himelf whether he is loved in return; when he
only knows that he loves and is moving to music—
then, and then only are two people able to dance perfectly in tune to the same rhythm.*

Ann Morrow Lindbergh, Gifts from the Sea

CLARA CODD

Another Side of Sex

The Sacred Science tells us that man and woman together
represent the twin creative forces of the universe, positive
and negative, centrifugal and centripetal, life in manifestation and life hidden. On the whole, man is positive, manifesting outwardly; woman is negative, receptive. But no
man is entirely masculine and no woman wholly feminine.
Medical science tells us that every man, physically, has
female attributes undeveloped within him, and every
woman has quiescent and undeveloped male characteristics. Sometimes when a sexual organ is removed the
secondary characteristics begin to develop, as witness the
feminity of the emasculated male, and the growth of masculine characteristics occurring sometimes in women whose
ovaries have been removed. There is also a period in fetal
life when it is a question which sex will finally predominate.

While one is paramount and visible, the other is always in the background, somewhat like the little man and woman who come out alternately on the weather gauge familiar to our childhood.

Men and women are not rivals, but co-operators, being entirely different in nature and outlook. To forbid one sex to use its peculiar powers and viewpoint in the life of the nation is like permanently closing one eye and expecting to see as well as with both.

As Lord Tennyson rightly wrote:

> For woman is not undeveloped man,
> But diverse . . .
> The woman's cause is man's; they rise or sink
> Together, dwarfed or godlike, bound or free.

COSMIC FORCES IN SEX DIFFERENTIATION

Man is not only a physical body. Closely knit and interpenetrating it, are other vehicles of consciousness composed of the subtler matter of surrounding, interpenetrating planes. Through these inner and outer bodies of man play forces which come down from the higher, subtler planes of being.

The eternal thing in matter is its ceaseless motion, the rhythmic ebb and flow of life. The most tremendous rhythm of all is the manifestation and apparent disappearance of the universe itself, called in the Indian scriptures: "Days and Nights of Brahma." The "nights," periods of non-manifestation, are caused by the final equalizing of all forces.

When a "day" dawns, the first principle to come into action is the Third Person of the Hindu Trinity, Brahman, the Divine Mind. "Brahma meditated and the worlds sprang into being." If God had not "thought" us into being, we should never have been. The same thing is true of our little worlds. Before we act, we think and therefore mentally create. During pralaya, or non-manifestation, spirit and matter, life and form, have become one as indeed they fundamentally always are. But during a "day" they draw apart and multiplication commences. This can be seen in the life of a cell. It has one nucleus, but when it is going to produce another cell two poles appear with a line between and presently there are two cells. "The One becomes Two." Here lies the real meaning of the old myth of the Virgin Birth, attached to nearly all world-saviours. In ancient writings spirit is spoken of as male, and matter as female, Mother-matter, in fact. In the undifferentiated state mare, the sea or noumenon of matter, is quiescent, one with life or spirit. When manifestation once more appears, this perfect equilibrium is disturbed. The first thrill or wave-length of the Divine Mind spreads through shoreless space. "The spirit of God moved upon the face of the waters." From that contact with virgin matter the Cosmic Son of God, the universe, was born.

The same miracle is repeated between man and woman. From their contact a "son of man" is born. The physical creative powers in man reflect the tremendous creative powers of Deity. Hence their extraordinary sanctity in the eyes of a simpler world of old. Because they are the highest physical powers in man their degradation produces terrible results. "Deus inversus demon est."

What for want of a better term we may call the positive force of the universe flows through the bodies of men, mostly along the lines of the bony and muscular system. Thus, we quite naturally consider the glory of a man to be his strength. But through the bodies of women the opposite force flows, mostly using the glandular and nervous system, and so we instinctively know that the glory of a woman is her grace. The attractive pull toward one another is clearly to be understood. The positive male principle forever seeks the more negative female principle, that both may be fulfilled and at rest. In a happy and successful marriage two effects are evident: one is the joy of creation, the other the sense of great rest. All creation is joy, not only physical creation, but the same power expressed mentally or spiritually. Archimedes, on his discovery of a scientific principle, rushed into the street, shouting with joy: "Eureka,

I have found it!" When God created the heavens and the earth all the sons of God shouted for joy, say the scriptures.

In the inner principles of man, constituting his subconscious or subjective self, the relation between the two sexes is reversed. On the emotional level woman is positive and man negative. Thus, the undeveloped woman is a mass of emotional contradictions, very possessive in her affections and when overstrained inclined to become hysterical. On the mental level the position is again reversed: man is positive, woman negative. The undeveloped man is inclined to be selfish and hard, a total unbeliever in anything not observed of the senses; the developed man has large and lucid powers of reasoning, and generally has a more impersonal outlook and greater creative powers of mind than a woman. But emotionally man is easily led. There is quite a touching element in a man's unspoiled love for a woman. He is so likely to worship, to look up to his goddess, to think her incapable of wrong. On the intuitive, spiritual levels woman again becomes predominant. The developed woman shines with intuitive wisdom and unselfish love. She has often a greater capacity for utter self-sacrifice than has a man. A woman in love is a natural devotee. Surrender and service are to her the supreme joy. Indeed, it may be said that to love and to be loved is the primal necessity of every woman's life. Byron knew this well, for he wrote:

> Love is of man's life a thing apart,
> 'Tis woman's whole existence.

The fact to be observed here is that the opposite, yet complementary factors involved in sex differentiation make them highly necessary and helpful to each other. Quite apart from any question of physical congress, the active intercourse of thought and action between the sexes is highly beneficial to both. The friendship of a man helps a woman to define her thoughts; the friendship of a woman inspires and warms a man's imagination. Therefore, we find that so many great men have had either a great wife or a great mother while other gifted men have fallen short of what they might have achieved, had they been blessed with this kind of association.

THE EXAGGERATED FACTOR

The world-wide prevalence of sex problems comes from the exaggeration of one factor in it, physical gratification. When physical gratification is the only, or the predominant, factor in a sex relationship it is passion and not love. It is as well to make a clear mental distinction between the two, for either can exist without the other, but where passion is exalted, purified and lit by love, physical union can take on a very beautiful and inspired meaning. While it gives the greatest physical pleasure known to man, it can also provide a channel for very exquisite and exalted emotion. Because the creative forces of the universe play through the oppositely polarized bodies of men and women there is an attraction between the two not equalled by any other for it is complemental and fulfilling, and therefore immensely satisfying. The beneficial effect of the inter-play of invisible magnetism already described becomes in the marital act greatly heightened, often breaking down mental barriers and enlarging the whole outlook of the participants. A happy and beautiful marital embrace can lead to what may only be described as a mystical experience, passing ever more deeply into an interior consciousness, so that the lovers become to each other as a door to God. This is known in India as a special form of yoga, called sahaja, leading to moksha, or liberation, through and by means of a certain attitude and relation possible to be established between lovers. This has nothing to do, say the sages, with the cult of pleasure. It is the realization of the One by the path of non-pursuit in love.

> All love greatens and glorifies
> Till God's aglow to the loving eyes
> In that which was mere earth before.
>   Robert Browning

This well-nigh perfect experience is extremely rare, as it demands such high and idealistic thinking on the part of the lovers, and such tremendous and true love. A great Egyptian Adept once wrote "Know, O Brother mine, that where a truly spiritual love seeks to consolidate itself doubly by a pure, permanent union of the two, in its earthly sense, it commits no sin, no crime in the eyes of the great Ain-Soph, for it is but the divine repetition of the Male and Female Principles—the microcosmal reflection of the first condition of Creation. On such a union angels may well smile! But they are rare, Brother mine, . . . Man's atma may remain pure and as highly spiritual while it is united with its material body; why should not two souls in two bodies remain as pure and uncontaminated notwithstanding the earthly, passing union of the latter two."

In the vast majority such a consummation is never reached. Far too often passion is unlit by love, far too often the husband regards the use of his wife's person as a physical convenience, and his right, eagerly and inconsiderately sought after and indulged in with very disastrous results. In the animal kingdom there are mating seasons and at all other times the mating urge is quiescent. Man, by virtue of his powers of memory and anticipation, has enormously heightened out of all natural order the sex impulse in himself. He is vulnerable to such impulses at all times.

The result is appalling. Let me quote *The Secret Doctrine* by Madame H. P. Blavatsky:

> The creative powers in man were the gift of Divine Wisdom, not the result of sin . . . Nor was the Curse of Karma called down upon them for seeking natural union, as all the mindless animal-world does in its proper season; but, for abusing the creative power, for desecrating the divine gift, and wasting the life-essence for no purpose except bestial personal gratification . . . In the beginning, conception was as easy for woman as it was for all the animal creation. Nature had never intended that woman should bring forth her young "in sorrow" . . . .
> For the seed of woman, or lust, bruised the head of the

seed of the fruit of wisdom and knowledge, by turning
the holy mystery of procreation into animal gratification;
hence gradually changing physiologically, morally,
physically and mentally, the whole nature of the Fourth
Race of mankind, until, from being the healthy king of
animal creation in the Third Race, man became, in the
Fifth, our Race, a helpless, scrofulous being and has now
become the wealthiest heir on the Globe to constitutional
and hereditary diseases, the most consciously and in-
telligently bestial of all animals! . . . This is the real Curse
from the physiological standpoint . . . The intellectual
evolution, in its progress hand-in-hand with the physical,
has certainly been a curse instead of a blessing—a gift
quickened by the "Lords of Wisdom" who have poured
on the human Manas the fresh dew of their own Spirit
and Essence. (Opus cited, 3rd revised edition, Vol. II,
pp. 428-429).

This was personified by the Greeks in the myth of Prometheus who brought the "fire" from heaven. Madame
Blavatsky continues (p. 430):

Prometheus answers:
Yea, and besides 'twas I that gave them fire.
Chorus: Have now these short-lived creatures flame-
eyed fire?
Prom.: Ay, and by it full many arts will learn.

But with the arts, the "fire" received has turned into the
greatest curse; the animal element, and consciousness of
its possession, has changed periodical instinct into
chronic animalism and sensuality. It is this which hangs
over humanity like a heavy funeral pall . . . The animal
world, having simple instinct to guide it, has its seasons
of pro-creation, and the sexes become neutralized during
the rest of the year. Therefore, the free animal knows
sickness but once in all its life—before it dies.

We read a good deal these days about sublimation, but
most of it seems to be vague or of little practical value.
Sublimation is possible, but its origin and rationale are not
understood. The truth is this: in all the universe there is
only one life and it is eternally creative. It flows through all

planes of matter and all phases of being. The Hindus call it
prana. Acting through our mental structure it stimulates
discovery, mental enquiry, creative thought. The "joy of
creation" here is the joy of discovery and invention. This is
why intellectual people often have less sexual urge than
many others. With them the creative force has taken
another direction. Emotionally the life stream shows as
admiration, love, ecstasy. Physically it exhibits as vitality,
especially in the creative sex function. The answer clearly
lies here. Increase the flow of the creative power on other
levels of being, and the pull upon the physical plane will
become less.

Free, intellectual enquiry and study, controlled living and
daily exercise are all contributing factors toward sex control, but the greatest of all lies in the emotional nature, and
in its higher counterparts, the spiritual and intuitional
principles. Modern man has lost his free, natural play of
feeling. He suffers from endless "suppressions," and these
date back in most cases to early childhood.

The greatest factor, however, is left unthought of and
undeveloped: the emotional nature. More than bread, more
than knowledge, a man's life depends upon the free, healthy
growth of his love and desire nature. The very word "emotion" shows its meaning, the motive force behind life. It is
necessary for man to love, to admire, to appreciate, to
generously share, to co-operate. Otherwise he cannot live
a happy and useful life. These qualities are the play of the
creative life in his emotional self, and if they are free and
beautifully grown, man has the finest sublimating force in
creation. The poets are well aware of this. So often the
poets teach us better than they know, better than the
philosophers. Wordsworth wrote:

> We live by admiration, hope and love,
> And even as these are well and wisely placed,
> In dignity of being we ascend.

Many people have forgotten how to exercise and express

their emotions. They feel that they do not love anything or anybody and that no one loves them. Suppressed in normal avenues, the emotional nature takes revenge by expressing itself in undesirable ways. If we have taught our children to love truly and to admire generously they will have little trouble with their sex natures in their later years.

Connected occultly with the emotional nature is the spiritual man, working on what is called the aspirational and intuitional level. There is a subtle connection between the two, hence the enduring bond between religion and sex. It lies in the fact that the creative impulse on the physical plane is the lower pole of that mystical, creative force which finally brings a soul into "union with God." Religion can be and is a potent means of sublimation.

Love, worship, adoration, appreciation: these are the real solvents. Many a married couple, joined by a sensual attraction only, can never forgive each other for being deprived of love and so that most dreadful thing of all, a deadly marital hatred, sets in.

THE QUALITY OF LOVE

Is love an "art" and can it be learned? From one standpoint we have really nothing else to learn. But love, true love, self-forgetting, generous, divine, is the product of slow growth and takes many incarnations to develop. It is both a science and an art, the eternal right and left hand of every potency. Science and religion, which latter is but the "artistic" approach to life, are not opposed to each other. The one but complements the other. The way of science is from below upwards, by patient, selfless investigation. The way of art is from above downwards, illuminating and inspiring the mind and heart with the shining down-flow of divine intuition. Each explains the other, but perhaps the divine flights of art pierce further into the supernal light than does the patient, steady tread of science, for, as George Sand put it: "The mind seeks, but it is the heart which finds."

Just as there is an art of worship to be learned in ever finer and nobler ways, so is there an art of love to be learned in ever higher and nobler ways of loving. A great lover is an artist indeed, and has won by sacrifice and sorrow this divine capacity. Like the poet, he is born and not made, and he is not so common a phenomenon as many people would suppose. Happy is the man who has this capacity; let him ask no other blessedness for within him is the "Light of the World." There is an old proverb which says that it is love which makes the world go around. Without love, indeed, which is the creative force of Deity in our souls, all things would cease to be. Descartes said: "I think therefore I am." Let us put it thus: "I love therefore I am." For he who does not love is already dead.

A relationship in life is a class in the school of love, teaching an angle of loving. To reap its full power we must not let the vice of selfish possession grip us. Jealousy is commonly supposed to be a sign of love, but it is only a proof of self-love. It is "natural," but we may grow out of the natural into the supernatural. In an ancient Tibetan scripture seven forms of love are enumerated, four belonging to the gods and three to men. The lowest of the three human forms is mere physical attraction, shared also by atoms and molecules. This exhausts itself as soon as satisfied. A higher form may be called psychic; it is on a reciprocal basis: I will love you if you will love me, and you owe me something for loving you. This form holds within itself the seed of its own death. The third form already borders on the ways of the gods and is a little difficult for men to achieve and so must generally be learned. This is to so love the beloved that we desire only his highest good and in his own terms. Such love is immortal and the ages cannot quench it. There is a tale of a devoted Indian wife who approached the Lord Buddha when He was upon earth to ask Him how she might be sure that she would be with her beloved husband in all future lives upon earth. The Blessed One replied that if she could be unfailingly faithful, tender and forgiving, she would bind his heart to hers for all lives to come.

Love in its highest sense is purified of egotism and many a heartbreak, many a loss, is to teach the soul this supreme secret. Immortal love is as the sun, shining upon the world because he is light, and asking nothing back. Possessiveness is an unexpurgated impurity, and so the heavenly bliss of true love cannot yet come, for only to the "pure in heart" opens the Divine Vision in all its wonder.

When sex is ennobled by love, it is purified, exalted; and can, as said before, become indeed a doorway to God, to the King in His beauty. How rare, how wonderful, how fine, must be the lovers to whom this comes! Yet it can come.

> Oh! world as God has made it, all is beauty,
> And knowing this is love, and love is duty,
> What further may be sought for or declared?
> Robert Browning

Just to love another as a source of personal satisfaction is what Madame Blavatsky called "égoisme à deux." Such love cannot endure. The vibratory wave between the two lovers must be closed, making a triangle. Love between man and woman has a curious quality; for itself alone it cannot live. It must be consecrated to and hallowed by a Higher than itself.

> I could not love thee, dear, so much
> Lov'd I not honour more.
> Richard Lovelace

And Plato wrote:

> Men have called Love Eros, because he has wings; the Gods have called him Pteros, because he has the virtue of giving wings.

One last word, *Love* must sanctify sex. Love, comradeship, mutual tolerance and consideration must begin to grow from the very early days of marriage, or a future wreckage is inevitable. Happy the couple who have made enduring friends with each other before the days of passion begin to wane. The great psychologist Carl Jung has said the same as the spiritual teacher Krishnamurti. Writes Jung: "When there is a sexual problem it can only be solved by love." And Krishnaji says: "There is no sex problem which cannot be solved by love." So once again, in the words of the old Latin saying: *Omnia vincit amor*, "Love conquers all."

13

Though the preponderance of male or female proper-
ties determines the sex in the higher forms of organic
life, each individual possesses simultaneously male
and female qualities. The higher the state of spiritual
development, the greater is the conscious interpene-
tration of male and female properties. The greatest
artists, poets, and thinkers are able to express with
equal perfection the psyche of man and woman,
which means that they are able to experience the
male and the female within themselves. The saint, the
holy one, i.e. the one who has become whole or com-
plete, has polarized the male and the female within
himself and attained a state of perfect harmony.
Lama Anagarika Govinda, Creative Meditation
and Multi-Dimensional Consciousness

ELISABETH HAICH

Sexual Energy in its False and True Light

In Revelation (5:6) we read how *logos* in the guise of a Lamb
with seven horns and seven eyes sets out to embody itself
in matter, to animate and spiritualize it and trace it back
to God:

> . . . and in the midst of the elders, stood a Lamb as it had
> been slain (in matter, in the body, the spirit feels as if it
> had been slain); having seven horns and seven eyes,
> which are the seven Spirits of God sent forth into all
> the earth.

And: "Behold the Lamb of God, which taketh away the sin
of the world." (St John I:29). "Taking away the sin of the
world" means for the spirit to assume the burden of the
attributes of matter. For the body, which is matter, the

112

attributes of matter are not sin; for the spirit, they are. The attributes, namely the laws of matter, are diametrically opposed to those of the spirit. In his Epistle to the Galatians (5:17-18) Paul says:

> For the flesh lusteth against the Spirit and the Spirit against the flesh: and these are contrary the one to the other: so that ye cannot do the things that ye would. But if ye be led of the Spirit, ye are not under the law (of the flesh, of matter).

The laws of matter are contraction, cooling, stiffening, hardening and solidification. The laws of the spirit are fire, warmth, heat, expansion and radiation. Therefore it is sinful for the spirit to manifest the attributes of matter. And in the same way it is sinful for matter to manifest the attributes of the spirit. The Lamb of God is spirit, and if it embodies itself in matter it must subject itself to the laws of matter and accept the attributes of matter, which for the Lamb are sin. Only in this way can *logos* spiritualize matter and trace it back to God.

The creative principle, *logos*, the Lamb of God, says of itself in another passage of the Bible: "*I* am the way, the truth, and the life: no man cometh unto the Father, but by me." (St John 14:6.) Thus the life that *I* myself am, in the very words of the *logos*, is itself the path by which we come to the Father. For this purpose life first embodied itself in matter, out of it formed a suitable shell, a body, and built into this body organs capable of begetting ever further bodies. The divine current of life flows uninterruptedly through these bodies, forming ever new shells, which become ever more able to bear and to manifest the vibrations of the spirit as resistance. And while the material, living and yet unconscious shell, the person, lives his shadowy existence, he is being wrought, indeed tormented, out of his unconscious mind by life, which in its materialized form is sexual energy, in order that his consciousness may be roused. In the individual, still unconscious part of his material being, primitive man's higher Self, *logos*, constantly impels him by means of sexual energy to become conscious in himself, in his material body, and to come to know the essence of his deepest being, God, that is to say, *to attain self-knowledge*. As long as man remains unconscious, he experiences God within himself as sexual desire. When he has become conscious, he experiences God as his own *Self*, as his own true being, as *I am!*—God is for man the absolute *state of self-awareness*.

In this way life, the eternal being, God, helps *itself* to grow more conscious in matter, in the body, till such time as the greatest miracle has been wrought: one and the same divine self-awareness embraces the opposing spiritual and material laws, matter is spiritualized, and in this spiritualized body the creative principle, *logos*, the Lamb of God which died into matter at birth, is at last resurrected after eons of development, and has again become itself, God. The Lamb and his wife, *logos* and the consciousness of the physical being have become *one*. The heavenly, mystical marriage has been performed!

Misunderstanding of the Scriptures and incorrect religious instruction have led Western man to regard the procreation of ever-new generations, without which life would cease, and the physical enjoyment and sensation of pleasure associated with this, as the work of the Devil. He has allowed the concept of "original sin" to be imprinted on his mind, and indeed to this very day regards the physical organs requisite to procreation as sinful and obscene. How admirably pure and divine is on the other hand the conception of some ancient and contemporary Asian peoples who regard the male genital organ, the Lingam, as sacred, and worship it as the outward material form of the divine, since its very purpose is to manifest and propagate the supreme: life, eternal being, God, through matter, through the body. It is naïve to a degree to suppose that the Orientals' worship of the Lingam involves worship of the merely physical male organ. Do they still believe in the West that antiquity and the Orientals who have achieved the supreme culture were and are so foolish as to worship a specific *member of the body*? The Orientals do not and have never worshipped matter or the body as such, but rather *the godhead manifesting itself* through the material form! Their entire philosophy of religion, their absolute disparagement of the physical clearly show this exalted mentality. Similarly, Western man is quite misled in seeing no more than mere pornography in the noble representations of the sexual act which adorn the majestic sun-god temples in Konarak, Bubaneshvar and other Indian temples. The inspired Indians who created these breathtaking, magnificent works of art did not regard the sexual act as obscene but as the imitation of the primal state of God, as the image of life, in which the two poles rest within each other and in which a new life, a new incarnation is made possible. They regarded the sexual act as the very deity which manifests itself through matter, separated into two halves, into two sexes but also reunited through the sexes to propagate earthly life in matter, so that the great aim may be achieved and realized, *to spiritualize matter, to attain divine self-awareness in matter, to experience the resurrection of human consciousness in God!*

It is a mystery how the white race has come to regard the sexual act which has given life to us and to our children as obscene and unmentionable. If it is something to be ashamed of why do the people who hold such views continue to perform it? And why then did God so create the world, according to these people, that this wicked act is absolutely necessary for the procreation of living creatures?

What a vast difference there is between the Eastern and the Western conceptions. On the one hand the Lingam is regarded as the embodiment of the forces of life and in it the divine is worshipped in order to beget children; on the other hand, the genital organ has been severed from the perfect, classical representations of Greek and Roman gods and the damaged parts covered with a vine or fig-leaf. (It is as if one had wished to attract even more attention to them.) Men who act in such a way betray their own sexual pathology. Instead of regarding the sexual act as an exalted fulfilment of the desire for oneness, for love, as a life-giving act in imitation of God, affording real contentment and happiness, they regard it as a brutish end in itself, good only for wanton and depraved sensual enjoyment, which has nothing whatever to do with love and true happiness. If these people thought differently, they would have no reason to cover up the genital organs as something obscene. By their own primitive mentality they cast the shadow of obscenity over the genital organs. These people drag the divine down into their own impurity. The fault lies, however, not in the divine, vitalizing force and sexual act, but in the attitude of those who so pervert these things that they have real cause to be ashamed. No wonder that the time had to come when the pendulum swung from prudery in the other direction. As a result there are today many pathological people who, on the one hand, attach excessive importance to sexuality by seeking a sexual cause for every mental disorder and, on the other hand, make light of sexual energy by provoking uninhibited sexual intercourse at every opportunity. As if sexual union were a cigarette to be smoked and then thrown away and forgotten! These people do not know that sexual energy is a manifestation of the *being of man* himself, and that there can be no sexual intercourse *without* conscious or unconscious *self-surrender.* The partner, whether male or female, is not an object to be used and discarded, but is a living creature and also has a human soul. This is true even of prostitutes! These misguided people try to satisfy their longing for happiness and mental stability by means of purely physical, sexual intercourse. People yearn for love, but not for purely physical gratification.

It is a dangerous error to seek love in soulless sexuality and to try to replace love by sexuality. It is natural enough for, say, women who are never given the slightest expression of love by their lifeless, uninteresting and uninterested "dead" husbands to believe that the tokens of tenderness shown by a husband interested in his wife during the brief period of sexual excitement constitute love and therefore to want to have sexual intercourse with their husbands as

often as they can. This is not because they are primarily interested in sexual intercourse as such, but because they
long for "a little bit of love." If the husband fails them, and
if an opportunity arises—which it nearly always does!—
they then try to get love from *another* man and to experience
sexuality to the full. In most cases they do not really do this
out of physical frustration. The body desires sexual gratification far less often than one imagines! Men long for
women to look up to them and admire them as the highest
manifestation of God, as man. If a man does not get this
recognition at home, he will certainly meet another woman
who pays him the tribute of admiration and afterwards it
usually looks as if he had only wanted sex. The man as well
as the woman looks for "love" from his or her lover but
they are wrong to believè that this is received from this
"other" partner. They meet secretly and, because they
always expect sexual intercourse, are in a state of sexual
excitement. And sexuality mimics love. It compels tenderness and embraces, it forces the lovers to hug one another,
to allay one another's pain through the revelations of
sexuality, as when true love is exchanged. What follows
such experiences? Disappointments, a bitter after-taste,
mutual accusations or bleak loneliness, and, in the case of
women, usually a desperate feeling of exploitation and de-
filement. *Neither of the two gave true love but only expected
to receive it, therefore neither received it!* Love can never
be replaced by empty, purely physical sexuality! And
humanity yearns, languishes for *love!* These countless poor
young souls, who are still little more than children and who,
largely because the "civilized" way of life is no longer conducive to love, perhaps went short of love from their
parents, give themselves up to sexual adventures and excesses because they are searching for *love!* The many
soul-sick people, young or old, can be healed only by love
and not by cheapening sexual intercourse or by wishing to
free them from sexual inhibitions and persuading them to
lead a dissolute, promiscuous and indiscriminate sex life.
How many of these people, young and old, seek advice on

how to regain their lost physical and spiritual purity after such irresponsible psychic treatment. And if one shows them only a little love and understanding, they return to life healed and ready to become useful members of society. We have not come across one of those people who suffered "repression" or "trauma" from the purity enjoined on them. By "purity" is meant of course not only a continent love-life, but also a healthy one based on *love*.

After the swing to extreme, indiscriminate "permissiveness" and false conceptions of sexual "freedom," caused by "repression" and "trauma," let us try to settle the pendulum in the middle and come to a normal conception of sexuality.

We should follow the example of great initiates who do not regard sexual energy as a malignant force but understand its secret and know that it is the sole means by which we human beings can attain the final goal—God. Here again the infinite wisdom with which entire creation is decreed reveals itself. Just as our ignorance alone brings us knowledge (see Elisabeth Haich: *Ein paar Worte über Magie*), so it is sexual energy alone which brings us liberation from itself, from sexual energy. Sexual energy frees us from the very sexual desires to which it gives rise again and again and leads us from mortality, from death, to redemption, resurrection, to LIFE.

The medieval alchemists, the Rosicrucians, depicted this process of development very cleverly: the sage makes the philosopher's stone by placing his tree of life in a washing-trough filled with the elixir of life. This is constantly heated by the fire of the dragon, sexual energy, to make the tree blossom.

Let us not therefore despise sexuality or regard it as the malignant force which reduces man to an animal, nor let us make of it such a force.

Let us look upon sexual energy as the key which opens the door for us between spirit and the world of matter, from the higher to the lower but also from the lower to the higher. Let us regard it, then, as the divine impetus which enables us to create further generations, to propagate life from above downwards in the body but also to transform man upwards out of his ferity into a spiritual man and to help to conquer death. We must be grateful that sexual energy, used properly, gives us so much happiness on both paths. On the downward path it is brief and transient, on the upward path it is eternal happiness.

Let us use its fire to make our tree of life flourish and blossom. Let us remember: primitive man is still at the lowest level of his consciousness. In his animal egoism he lives within himself completely isolated and immured; his heart is still dead and he still has no inkling of the meaning of love. Sexual energy, that elemental fire, is alone able to warm his dead heart for the first time. And even if during the brief spell of sexual excitement he can experience and express only an inkling of love, it is notwithstanding the first glimmer of divine love. Through sexuality he first becomes acquainted with the happiness derived from giving. And although his dawning love is still no more than an animal desire, a passion, his excitement is, even if only quite unconsciously and briefly, already an urge towards oneness, towards love! Even if at first he experiences this urge towards love only in the body and hence can only look for *physical* gratification, it is nevertheless the first reflection of spiritual oneness in the great Self, which man is unconsciously seeking and which, after long development, perhaps over eons, he will find because he is destined to do so. Sexual energy causes us inner unrest which never allows us to stand still. It continually spurs us on and compels us to find the inner path after many wanderings. In an unexpected moment, among the animal impulses, in the "night," in the darkness of unconsciousness, our self-awareness is born, just as the Holy Child was born in a manger, among animals, in the "night," in darkness. And man sets out on the great path, he decides to journey from the first awakening of consciousness in the Self to the paradisiacal universal consciousness, to the goal. And as he gradually grows conscious in himself on this long path, so there unfolds within him the ability to control creative energy in all its manifestations and to use it in accordance with his will. If he once reaches the highest level, the source of divine power, he will be able to transform the lower forms of energy of divine creative power into their higher forms and with the higher spiritual forms of energy he will be able to control and guide the lower forms and to manifest all of these energies through the corresponding nerve centres. Let us come to know this divine power, let us try by its help to climb higher on Jacob's ladder, and by so doing, help sexual energy to transform itself into its higher vibrations, into spiritual power. Where there is consciousness, creative power is at work.

14

For spirits when they please can either sex assume, or both, so soft and uncompounded is their essence pure.
John Milton, Paradise Lost

GINA CERMINARA

Sex in the Edgar Cayce Readings

At first glance it may seem a bit incongruous to associate so dramatic a subject as sex with so theoretical a subject as reincarnation; but in actuality there may be a very vital and very important connection between the two.

This connection first became apparent to me when I was studying the clairvoyant records of Edgar Cayce. As many people know, Cayce gave a strange kind of study, called a life reading, on many hundreds of people. These readings constituted a kind of psychoanalysis of the persons in question, with these significant differences from the usual psychoanalysis: 1) they were given while Cayce was lying on a couch rather than the person being analyzed; 2) they were frequently given with distances of many miles between Cayce and the person being analyzed, on the basis merely of a name, address, and birth date; and 3) they accounted for the present-life situation in terms of some past-life causation.

While these readings have their own limitations, they certainly do add important evidence for the validity of clairvoyance as a faculty of the human mind; and while they cannot fairly be said to constitute proof of reincarnation, they at least provide a kind of circumstantial evidence.

Certainly the case histories of all these hundreds of people do give the theory of reincarnation a new immediacy. Coming upon them with a background in Theosophical thought and some knowledge of Hinduism and Buddhism, I myself felt as if, to the skeleton of a hypothesis, I suddenly saw the addition of flesh, muscle, nerve currents, and the throbbing pulsation of life.

Sex is, as any student of advertising and publishing knows, a highly intriguing phenomenon, charged with explosive possibilities and accompanied by an infinite number of strange, beautiful, and terrible ramifications. With it are involved the most intense of human emotions: love, hate, jealousy, treachery, betrayal, cruelty, sacrifice, devotion. Suicide and murder frequently take place because of it. Life is brought into being as its consequence. Lives are dramatically and drastically changed through its agency. Little wonder, then, that sex has been the endless thematic source for poetry, song, drama, and literature of every kind in every age.

As with all other realms of human life, the reincarnation idea enables us to see sex on a far wider screen of vision, and at the same time makes clear and reasonable matters that otherwise would seem chaotic and senseless.

To find oneself in a human body is to find oneself either male or female. This curious circumstance not only makes life more interesting; it also makes it more complicated. It seems that all of us have been men in some lifetime and women in others. At least, sex change is generally accepted as a fact by most believers in reincarnation, such as Buddhists, Hindus, Theosophists, Rosicrucians, and others; and the Cayce readings, as well as the age-regression experiments of many investigators, provide confirmation for those who accept their validity.

No regular pattern of change is deducible from the Cayce data, however; it seems that one can be a man for one or more lifetimes and then a woman for one or more lifetimes, and so forth and so on; but what causes such changes, or when they occur, does not become clear by the Cayce data at least. But the mere fact that we *do* change is itself of epoch-making significance, psychologically speaking.

In *Many Mansions* we saw how, by the continuitive aspect of karma, talents are carried over from one life to another; how attitudes towards race, religion, politics, and the opposite sex can persist from life to life also. These attitudinal carry-overs can be general: as, for example, hatred for religion in general, or sympathy for the underdog; or they can be very specific: as, for example, love for or hatred for some specific individual.

The carry-overs persist despite the change in sex in the individuals involved, or despite the changed role in a family situation or otherwise. Two brothers who became enemies in the past, for example, because one of them won the girl that both of them loved, were born as father and son this time, and a bitter hostility characterized their relationship from the very beginning.

Attitudinal carry-overs such as this could explain many otherwise incomprehensible antagonisms and sympathies among people, and particularly so in the marriage or the sex relationship.

There would seem to be, moreover, a certain temperamental polarity that is basic to many human relations and especially to the sex relationship, both because of biological and cultural factors that have existed for many ages. A theory of the psychologist William McDougall can be very instructive in this connection.

McDougall, in an attempt to account for the manic-depressive psychosis, argues that there are two basic innate modes of response typical of all human beings: (1) the self-assertive and (2) the self-submissive. An individual reacts submissively with regard to his parents, shall we say, assertively with regard to his wife, submissively with regard to his employer, and assertively with regard to his dog. The normal person is able to make all these adjustments of attitude with the same fluency with which he would go from one gear to another in driving his car. If, however, he tends to act submissively with regard to all persons and all situations, or if, instead, he tends to act always with extreme self-assertion, he is going dangerously in the direction of abnormality.

The manic-depressive psychosis is, according to Mc-Dougall, a form of breakdown occasioned when the individual, through either of these exaggerated tendencies or through rigidity in making natural transitions from one to the other, has lost touch with reality. His mental illness then proceeds with exaggerated bounds from the depths to the heights of emotion, in excessive swings from self-submission to self-assertion, thus revealing, as so many abnormalities do, the normal mechanism on a magnified scale.

We are not at present concerned with manic-depressive psychosis, or with the truth or falsity of this theory or its origins; but McDougall's division of basic disposition into self-assertive and self-submissive is extremely interesting and extremely helpful in analyzing the Cayce data having to do with the relations between the sexes.

In modern America, of course, women have an unprecedented economic freedom and independence. There still does not exist full equality of the sexes, even in America; but such rapid strides are being made in this direction, there are so many career women and there is so much self-assertion among women that it seems almost absurd to say —even remembering her biological role—that the role of woman is one of self-submission.

But we must bear in mind that this economic liberation, and the democratic ideal of equality between the sexes, is of very recent and even almost regional growth. Only fifty years ago in this country it was impossible for women to vote; and there are still millions of women all over the world whose condition is essentially the ancient one of submission rather than assertiveness. In the light of these facts, it seems safe to say that the basic disposition of self-assertiveness has, throughout much of human history, been equated with the male, and self-submissiveness with the female. Sadism can be regarded as the extreme of ruthless self-assertiveness; masochism, the extreme of self-submission.

If, then, we see by the reincarnationist view that one's sex and one's role in life are constantly changing, we can see that the permutations and combinations of assertiveness and submissiveness must lead to many curious psychological situations. Such situations in the marriage relationship, in fact, appear frequently in the Cayce readings.

There are many cases in the Cayce files where a husband and wife in the present have been in the relationship of father and daughter before. These antecedents, observable in dozens of cases, sometimes have favorable and sometimes unfavorable consequences. In general, such a situation seems to be favorable to marital harmony, because the pattern of dominance-submission which is typically that of a parent-child situation is identical with the traditional culture pattern of dominance-submission in the husband-wife relationship.

In the following case, for example, we see a favorable consequence. The woman in this case is the daughter of a famous American writer, and the widow of a distinguished European artist. She asked in her life reading whether she had been united with her husband in previous lives. She was told: "More than once. In the Danish experience, he was only a friend. In the Egyptian experience, he was your father. In Atlantis, he was your husband." The woman writes, in a letter acknowledging the receipt of her reading, "I was very much impressed by the statement that in a previous incarnation my husband had been my father, because there was a certain element of that quality in our relationship even in this life."

It should be noted here that the attitude of self-submissiveness which was deeply ingrained in the Egyptian parent-child experience persisted through the less emotionally charged experience of friendship in Denmark and came down to the present as a continued sense of the woman's looking upward as to a superior. It is also of interest to note that the woman in this case was four years *older* than her husband, so that one might almost have expected a motherly attitude on her part rather than a daughterly one.

In other cases, however, the unconscious pattern of parent-child relationship was one of antipathy rather than sympathy (because of a tyrannical element in the dominance); the results in the present husband-wife relationship were, therefore, unfortunate. One case is that of a Polish-born woman who asks: "What has been my relationship in the past with my husband? Why have I feared him?" The answer was: "In the Mohawk Valley experience there was an association as father and daughter; he then kept the entity well in tow." Another case is that of a marital relationship so difficult as to result in a nervous breakdown on the part of the wife. The husband's attitude had constantly been one of cold domineering tyranny, which took subtle rather than obvious forms. According to their readings, they were father and daughter in early Williamsburg, and the stern authority of the parent then was fiercely resented by the child. The pattern of domineering tyranny on the one hand, and resentment on the other, never relented into consideration on his part, nor forgiveness on hers; consequently, the same situation had to be met again, though in a slightly different form.

An interesting case of a previous mother-son relationship is to be seen in the case of a famous and wealthy American industrialist who was refused a divorce by his wife for many years. Unable to win his freedom, he proceeded to live with and support another woman with whom he had a deep bond of sympathy and understanding, a woman of quick intelligence and wide culture. She was his confidante in matters of business and was solicitous both of his health and his tastes in food. She was told: "In the Atlantean sojourn, he was the son of the entity. And the whole of the relationship in the present often bears just that same aspect, as the entity mothers his ideas and his welfare."

Frequently a husband and wife were previously associated in exactly the same husband-wife relationship. This exact repetition of role is apparently very common. If the dominance-submission pattern or the equality pattern has been well established by such previous marriages, the present marriage adjustment is very probably a relatively harmonious one. No conflict of attitude polarity is likely to arise unless other disturbing factors or karmic problems are present. There is no need, then, to dwell on these cases at any length here, though we might note in passing one rather curious case. The woman was told by Cayce that she had been traded in marriage in early Virginia for 2,000 pounds of tobacco. When she asked about her previous relationship with her husband, she was told, "He was the one who bought you! Doesn't he act like it at times?" The wife's comment on this was simply: "He sure does!"

In many cases, a previous male incarnation of the wife militates against successful marriage. This is very distinctly observable in the case of a woman who was united with her present husband in the same relationship several lifetimes ago. In the life just previous to the present one, however, she took incarnation as a man. From this male incarnation she carries over a very pronounced desire for domination and independence, together with a man-like strength of purpose that will brook no opposition. Their present marriage has been one of continuous strife almost from its inception. The partners have divorced and remarried twice. The excessive drinking, which has become the weakness of both, is a symptom as well as a contributing factor to their friction. Basically, one major difficulty is the pronounced self-assertive tendencies of both. If one or the other, or both, could achieve sufficient grace of spirit for a sufficiently long period of time to curb his own self-assertive attitude and be patient of the eruptions of self-assertion in the other, the marriage could perhaps be salvaged.

In other cases we see the reverse situation: namely, one in which the husband has made a recent change in sex, and consequently has a tendency to be feminine and self-submissive in outlook. In one case, for example, that of a somewhat effeminate man who is the father of three children and suffers acutely from sexual maladjustment, the Cayce reading indicated that he had had two previous lives as a woman, one in early America and one in France during the Crusades. The Crusade experience was particularly traumatic; the entity had been betrothed as a young girl to a man who soon afterwards went to the Holy Land. "Knowing little or nothing of the duty of matrimony, the entity's whole experience was filled with suppression and fear of sexual relationships. The entity was well on in years before these fears were removed."

We have, of course, only skimmed the surface of this whole area. The Cayce files contain any number of cases illustrative of one or another of the many possible permutations of sexual role, as do the files of Mr. Loehr and Dr. Baker also.

The basic fact of sex transposition is of importance, first, as an explanation for many strange undercurrents in human relations, particularly as related to love and hate, dominance and submission; and second as an indication to us of the cosmic lesson that we all need to learn.

Life seems almost to be like a school for actors: the director of the school wishes each student to be so flexible and so complete, as to be able to play *all* roles equally well, and for this purpose makes everyone, willy-nilly, play widely different parts, no matter what his natural inclinations. Were you superb as Puck last night? Very well, then, tomorrow you must begin to learn the role of Shylock. Were you magnificent as a man last life? Very well, then, next life you must learn to be a woman.

In psychological terms, we must learn to be neither too self-assertive nor too self-submissive with regard to other people, no matter what our role in life. No matter what opportunity for dominance presents itself as an enticement and justification to our ego, no matter what situation of oppression seems to overwhelm us into slavery and insignificance, we must learn to be as unaffected by the one as by the other.

To our temporary inferiors, we must fulfill our responsibilities of leadership or instruction or support; to our temporary superiors, we must act with due respect, obedience, or compliance; but in the former case we must not become unduly self-exalted, and in the latter case we must not become unduly self-abased.

The abrasions and agonies of marriage are intended to polish us of our crudities, bring to the surface our latent strengths, teach us to become more self-assertive if we are too self-submissive, or to become more self-submissive if we are too self-assertive.

Positivity and negativity are complementary parts of the whole universe and of God himself. To become godlike, then, and universal, we must become both positive and negative; we must become completely androgynous.

In this, as in all other respects, the purpose of the universe is that we shall become justly poised above, as the *Bhagavadgita* puts it, the Pairs of Opposites; bestride, in Madame Blavatsky's profoundly gnostic phrase, the Bird of Life. . . .

Part III

The Religious Perspective

This third and last section centers upon religious and philosophical views of love and sex. The role of love of God and the notion of chastity as a virtue in marriage is discussed in the context of Christianity and Judaism. Also, the concept of loving not so much the outer appearance but the divine or "real" person is seen as a viable path to renewed interest and vigor in relationships. This concept derives from Eastern views, which have become increasingly popular and accepted in the West. Three of the articles are explicitly from an Eastern point of view.

In this section sex is depicted as a part of spiritual discipline, which may be practiced by those who wish. However, this is not the sex of passion and desire only; it is the sex of the man or woman who wants to turn everything to the Divine, who sees Divine Immanence in all life. Maleness and femaleness are seen as divine in their own right and a means for self-transcendence. Sex is a part of the manifestation of the Creator, and men and women are creators in a universe that is divine "play."

Finally, union in sexuality, though truly a unifying coming together, is seen as a symbol for any union: a meeting of minds in a close or intimate way, an intuitional sharing of the beauty of a sunset, or the union of the spiritual energy in the universe with the physical world.

15

For even as love crowns you so shall he crucify you.
Even as he is for your growth so is he for your pruning.
Even as he ascends to your height and caresses your
tenderest branches that quiver in the sun
So shall he descend to your roots and shake them in
their clinging to the earth.

Kahlil Gibran, The Prophet

GEDDES MACGREGOR

A Christian Approach to Sex and Love

Christian marriage is uniquely beautiful and creative, especially when it has matured into the indestructible relationship that has gradually developed between two lovers who have made the engagement out of a deep and true love for one another and at the same time out of a profound commitment to God. Christians believe it to be the most holy and blessed relationship that can exist between a man and a woman on this earth. It entails the recognition of the ideal of chastity, which is anything but a popular concept in today's world. It is nevertheless not only a noble ideal but, when properly understood, a practical and productive one that brings unparalleled joy. From a Christian stance it not only implies sacrifice; it is utterly impossible apart from the kind of relationship to God that is envisioned in the Household of Faith as the fundamental condition of Christian

133

marriage. To understand it, therefore, we must both look at the situation today and then glance at the historical background of Christian attitudes to sex and love that are the underpinnings of what has made possible the spiritual richness of the contemporary Christian attitude and aim.

Christians believe they have access to a special dimension of spirituality in marriage. They think of this dimension not only as investing a romantic relationship with a sacred character but as invoking the power of God so to bless it that the parties will grow in such a way as to bind them indissolubly to one another and to God. That is expressed in the simple aphorism: "It takes three to get married." In the Christian marriage ceremony the couple, when they engage in their solemn vows, perform the marriage ceremony in the presence of the priest or minister who stands as a symbol of the divine Christ without whom such a sacred marriage is impossible.

This approach is a realistic one, whatever else it is. Every young couple in love feels sure that their feeling of love will last forever; yet no young couple can possibly know this. No man or woman on earth, however passionate, however sincere, and however deep his or her love may be, can promise to have even next year, let alone forty years hence, the same *feeling* for the beloved that we all feel when we fall in love. The Christian expectation is not that a couple will always "*feel* the same" about one another; the Christian expectation is that they will so mature through the bond that they have with Christ and his Church that the *quality* of their love will deepen beyond all they can possibly now know. In the relationship into which they are entering, sexual passion, fundamental though it be, is only one element. That must surely be obvious. But even the element of romantic love that accompanies and adorns sexual passion is no less ephemeral and much more delicate. In any marriage relationship the partners are juggling with an array of elements whose full power and strength they cannot possibly know. If a marriage has nothing more to it than mutual consent, however sincere, its chance of surviving for even ten years as a genuinely deep mutual relationship is about as slim as that of their being hit by a meteorite on their way to work. For everything is against the success of any marriage that lacks the God-dimension.

What the Christian couple do, if they have been well counseled, is to enter into a sacred undertaking so to grow in wisdom and goodness under the grace and power of God that their marriage will withstand the inevitable stresses to which all marriage by its very nature is exposed. These stresses arise both from external circumstances and from their own personal immaturity and inexperience in handling so difficult a relationship as the lifelong bond in which Christian marriage consists.

The dangers that hover around every marriage are legion. Nor do they by any means consist merely in the pretty girl next door or the handsome visitor to town. The American dream of social status and real estate with the overspending that is the inevitable accompaniment of such rainbow-chasing almost assures failure *even apart* from the triangle that is the stock-in-trade of the popular novelist and film-maker. The anxiety that such approaches to life may create in the man, even when the wife helps in the breadwinning process, sometimes results in his sexual impotence, sometimes even in his premature death. There are more causes of marriage breakdown than could ever be calculated. What *is* calculable is the divorce rate. In the United States *at least* one marriage in three ends in divorce; in California the ratio is nearer two out of three. Affluence is an aggravating condition. In New Testament times and indeed till about a century ago life for most people was on the whole very much harder than it is for even the poorer classes today. Yet human nature has changed little in the course of two thousand years. That is, after all, a very brief span in human history. Marriage simply does not work without the God-dimension. It is difficult enough even with it.

The teaching of Jesus and Paul is clear on at least one point: marriage is not merely a sacred bond; it is a metaphor for the relationship between God and his people. This is expressed in the introduction to the marriage service. Christian marriage, then, is not merely a partnership agreement such as two friends or professional associates might enter into. It is not even the sanctification of such an agreement. It is a covenant to continue to beseech God so to bless the relationship that both the man and the woman grow into each other *in God*. The one cares for the other through thick and thin and always in the sight of God. It is, as the marriage service expressly states, a mystical union. The parties to a Christian marriage undertake not only fidelity to a person; they promise fidelity to a holy institution that celebrates their mystical union with God.

Divorce plainly stands in absolute contradiction to the basic concept of Christian marriage. This is enunciated in Mark 10.1 and Luke 16.18. To this Matthew 5.32 seems to provide a qualification; but its interpretation is highly controversial and the issues are too technical and complex to be considered here. But there is no doubt that divorce, which was merely tolerated in the Mosaic law (Deuteronomy 24.1-4), was from the beginning detested in the Christian Household of Faith. Yet forgiveness is central to Christian behavior. In a relationship so sacred to the Christian community as well as to the partners, a Christian whose spouse has committed any offense against the marriage, even adultery, should be ready to forgive the other, who should likewise be able to accept the forgiveness. I have known marriages in which such forgiveness has so strengthened the marriage bond and so developed the maturity of the partners (not least the forgiving one) as to have made the marriage thenceforth seemingly indestructible. Forgiveness is peculiarly holy. Nevertheless, anything that injures the other party to a Christian marriage is always a matter of extreme remorse. Divorce, if it is to be tolerated at all, must be regarded as a last resort. It is at best a lamentable option. Chesterton's observation that what is needed is not easier divorce but more difficult marriage applies with superlative force to Christian marriage.

When a young Christian couple fall in love they are beset

by a vast array of pressures, some arising from their own sexual impulses, some from the world at large, and some from the constraints of the Church, which usually includes their own immediate families. Typically, their families urge caution and restraint (the dispositions that usually seem least to the young couple's liking), for what a young couple in the storm of sexual passion calls "falling in love" is likely to be a poor foundation (to say the least) for an enduring marriage of the kind a Christian parent wants for his or her family. From any Christian standpoint no marriage that lacks the foundation necessary to mature into a lifelong union is worth contracting. By any reckoning, Christian marriage is so sacred, so demanding, so sacrificial, that it must be intended from the first to be indissoluble except by death. Spiritually it is a union that should become so joyous and so morally exigent that no young couple on earth can be said to be mature enough to engage in it, were it not for belief in the gracious guidance of God. If their faith is lively enough they may and inevitably will do so. What are the conditions of success in so hazardous an enterprise?

We have seen that the hazards are indeed tremendous. When the overwhelming pressure of the sexual impulse is combined with the natural desire and need for loving companionship, young people in the Christian Household of Faith tend to be stricken with the same exuberant confidence that young couples in love have always felt everywhere and at all times in human history: they feel sure their love can overcome all obstacles. If they are churchgoing Christians they may additionally feel assured that their common faith will carry them through. They rarely if ever reckon with the devastating effect that even the most trivial, the most ridiculously minor irritations can have on the most promising of marriages.

The triviality of the irritations can be truly astounding to even the most experienced of marriage counselors. A young wife once confided to me that her husband of three months had not told her before their marriage that he wore glasses.

Was not this, she wondered aloud, a deception? A young husband complained that, when his wife's brother had been hurt in an automobile accident, she had taken him home from the scene of the accident without first consulting her husband. There is no end to the absurd triviality of the problems adduced, and usually, of course, they are not the real problems at all. The fundamental problem is usually a lack of emotional, moral, and spiritual maturity on the part of one spouse or the other, very often of both.

The purpose of Christian marriage has two dimensions: (1) to foster mutual fellowship, encouragement, and understanding, and also, where possible, the procreation of children and their physical and spiritual nurture; and (2) to sustain the Household of Faith in its resistance to the World, the Flesh, and the Devil, in accordance with the baptismal vows taken by or on behalf of every candidate for Christian baptism. So the couple who seek Christian marriage are required to make their utmost effort to establish the relationship with God's help. The fact that they undertake to establish it implies that the relationship is not yet present; neither is it instantly achieved by the marriage ceremony any more than does the sacrament of Baptism instantly produce holiness of life. Like a tender sapling the relationship is planted in the rich soil of the Christian community; but it must be tended. It must be watered with sacrificial love and opened daily to the sunshine of God. It does not come ready-made; it must grow. The notion that it is an entirely private affair that is nobody else's business is a thoroughly secular notion at enmity with Christian marriage, since on the contrary the Christian Household of Faith has a creative and constructive part to play, however discreetly it should play it. Moreover, the two individuals who enter into this relationship are themselves growing as individuals. Their individual growth may conflict with the growth of the relationship; yet if they have been serious about their marriage they will each do all possible so to sustain and develop the marriage as to deepen it week by week, month by month, year by year. It is an extremely delicate kind of nurture that is called for. Neither men nor women have the natural talent for it that they often suppose. Generally they make a mess of it. That is one of the reasons why in Christian marriage they must constantly turn to God for guidance. Christian marriage is an incessant duet of prayer to God.

The marriage vows are "for better, for worse, for richer for poorer, in sickness and in health, to love and to cherish, till death do us part." That is not a promise that his feelings for her and hers for him are to remain exactly what they were when he first found her lips irresistible and she went crazy at the sound of his voice. It is a pledge that nothing shall ever come between them or separate the one from the other save only death itself and even death shall not undo the holiness of their relatedness.

The worst possible preparation for such a solemn and beautiful and holy undertaking is premarital promiscuity. The ideal of chastity is as relevant to happiness today as ever it was in the past. We instinctively know this, whatever the doctrinaire interpreters of Freud may wish us to believe. Bedhopping stunts the growth of true love and in the long run breeds selfcentered and lonely women and men. Of course in the heat of passion young people will always be in danger of slipping and we all stand in need of forgiveness; but if only the beauty and the holiness of the Christian marriage ideal is kept constantly alive in their hearts they will be sowing the seed therein for the growth of the loveliest and most firm of all human relationships.

Then when the couple enter into marriage they will have been already prepared for the innumerable challenges that must come to them; for instance, one feels the other has behaved unlovingly, perhaps even insultingly. A storm ensues. Christian marriage provides no promise that the partners will not fight. Of course they will. The best and holiest of marriages are often the most stormy. What is undertaken is that no fight shall ever separate them from the love of God and their fidelity to one another. So such storms will subside in the loving presence of God and leave them bound more inextricably than before in the ever-growing love that is God's gift to all who enter into the holy bond of marriage. "The family that prays together stays together" may sound a jingoistic catchphrase; but it is true. When husband and wife have a little prayer in their hearts, if not on their lips, every morning and night, it will help immensely to keep their marriage growing from the delicate young shoot it is into the great tree it can become. Of course children, when a marriage is blessed with them, can rivet the marriage bond; nevertheless some of the happiest marriages I have seen have been between childless couples who have grown old together without this blessing. What matters most for marital happiness is a constant immersion of human love in the pool of God's mercy and care.

HISTORICAL BACKGROUND

To understand more fully the Christian emphases on this subject and how these emphases have developed over the centuries, some treatment of the history of Christian attitude to marriage can be illuminating.

The Christian Way from the first demanded sexual restraint, partly by way of showing a good example to the pagans among whom the Christian communities were growing up in an environment of notable sexual license (excavations and restoration at Corinth show that the brothel stood almost opposite the library), partly in the belief (by no means unique to Christianity) that sexual abstinence is intrinsically conducive to spiritual growth. If some degree of sexual restraint is spiritually productive, must not lifelong continence be much more so? That has been the traditional Catholic view. It has biblical warrant. It is as strong in the Eastern as in the Western Church, for although Greek parish priests are permitted to marry, they may marry only before their ordination and if they become widowed they may not re-marry; moreover, bishops must be celibate and are therefore usually selected from the monks, who of course are celibate. In the early Church, rigorous rules about Christian behavior prevailed, according to which no person who had been baptized and found guilty of any of a list of grave sins such as murder could ever again be restored to the Christian Household. Adultery was one of the sins on the list. In these and in many other ways we can see that sexual activity of any kind was generally regarded as animal behavior, not seemly in those committed to the Christian Way, although permitted within strict limits for the perpetuation of the human race. Some, such as the followers of Marcion in the second century, urged total sexual abstinence with a view to the non-perpetuation of the human race and the "end of the age." Marcion and his followers were, however, condemned as heretical. On the mainstream view, sexual activity could be approved where it could be shown to have, at least theoretically, a purpose.

One must bear in mind that the traditional Christian attitude toward sexuality often tended to look a middle-of-the-road approach between the fanatical Manichaean extremists on the one side, who accounted all sexual expression as essentially evil and a capitulation to the forces of Satan, and the libertines on the other side who in every age seek to promote anarchy in sexual mores and promiscuity under pretense of freedom. In terms of the knowledge and ignorance of the age the Church's attitude toward sexuality was both more restrained than it is commonly depicted by those who taunt it with sexual depravity and more humane than it is generally presented by those who accuse it of cruel repression.

What was almost totally absent in the medieval attitude to sexuality was the romantic element and the concept of deep friendship that we nowadays take for granted as distinctive of any civilized attitude toward sex. Marriage was conceived in extremely legalistic terms, focused on the vows made in the marriage ceremony and therefore the fulfilment of a binding legal contract. We hear much about the effect of the chivalric ideal on medieval attitudes toward sexuality; but in fact that ideal affected only a small elite and even there more as a literary conceit than anything else. Such influence as it exerted was only very slowly developed and until the nineteenth-century romantic revival its results were comparatively meager. The Beatrice of Dante's *Commedia* and the knight's lady in troubadour verse bore almost no relation to anything in actual practice. Nevertheless, the chivalric notion did present a new model and with it the seeds of a fresh Christian understanding of sexuality, although the seeds took long to germinate.

With this fresh attitude has gradually been developed a more positive understanding of the nature of the virtue of chastity. On the old model, not least under the influence of a half-baptized Aristotelianism, chastity was seen in almost entirely negative terms as abstinence from sexual activity. Gradually, through a variety of enlightening influences, Christians have come to see it as a positive form of virtue. Sexuality, like the other constituents of our being, is polar, having roots both in our bodies and in our minds; but its mental aspect is crucially important. Of course Christians in the ancient world and in the Middle Ages often perceived all this in their own way, the mystics preeminently; but it was largely ignored in the Church's official teaching. They knew in their own way that the power of human sexuality lies, for good or ill, in the mind even more than in the body; but they had no rationale such as we can provide today to justify such an outlook. Similarly, they saw in their own way the enormous difference between men and women; but they misunderstood what the difference is. Their ignorance of sperm cells and ova contributed of course to that misunderstanding; but much more so did their widespread lack of the psychological insights that we take for granted today. Such insights had been writ deep into the Ancient Wisdom in one way or another but were lost in the maze of medieval legalism.

THE ANDROGYN MYTH

Three Greek terms are used that may all be translated "love." They are: *erōs, philia,* and *agapē.* The first of these is familiar in classical usage. It means fundamentally "desire." Its meaning has been debased in the modern use of the term "erotic" for mere ruttishness lacking in debonair joy of mind. The second term, *philia*, generally signifies the kind of love that springs from human friendship and is spiritually ennobling. The New Testament term *agapē*, which the King James translator somewhat unfortunately rendered "charity," is used to signify that peculiarly altruistic love that transcends self-interest. Of course all forms of love have an element of self-interest in them and in even the crudest sexual love is at least a germ of altruistic concern for the partner to the love. The tenderness that we expect in the love-making of civilized people is an expression of such altruistic concern, apart from which sexuality remains at a bestial level.

On a Christian view, maintenance of the sharp distinction between the sexes provides a means for the development of that altruistic element in love that invests it with deep spirituality. Hence the emphasis upon the sanctity of marriage and the commitment of the partners to marital fidelity. Built into the altruism, however, is also the ability and the willingness to forgive, for if the Christian has reached anything like the standard set forth so magnificently by Paul in the thirteenth chapter of his first letter to the Corinthians, he or she will apply it not least in his or her attitude to the marriage partner, who is no longer seen either as a chattel or as a despot but as partner in a spiritual development that lifts men and women, through the sexuality they have in common with other mammals, up to the fulfilment of their fundamentally spiritual nature.

But what of the androgynous element in sexuality of which modern psychoanalysis, not least the Jungian sort, has made so much? In every male psyche is at least a vestige of femininity and in every female one at least a particle of masculinity. What is accounted masculine or feminine is to a great extent a matter of social custom. In one society men wear sombre clothes and the use of color in dress is distinctively feminine, but as is the case in some other species the situation might be the very opposite. That we may easily change roles has long been recognized. Edward Young (1683-1765) writes:

> Sometimes, through pride, the sexes change their airs;
> My lord has vapours, and my lady swears.

Yet so ingrained are our images that we even call cities masculine or feminine: Paris is said to be the latter and London the former. What comes to be dubbed masculine and what feminine is to a considerable extent so by arbitrary social convention, although one cannot get past biological differences in the way in which men and women are physically constructed. A male whose mind contained, however, no vestige of those sensibilities that are conspicuous in the female psyche would be a monster, as would be that of a woman totally bereft of masculine elements. The former would be a brute and the latter a lace doyley. Yet to cultivate "unisex" aims is to deprive human beings of one of the most powerful means for the development of that altruism on which spirituality depends. According to the myth of the androgyn, sexuality is the result of the separation of the two halves of what had been archetypally a unity. There is no way, however, in which, at our present level of consciousness on this planet, an individual can attain an androgynous status. A "unisex" society would be the antithesis of a Christian one for more than one reason but especially because of the selfcenteredness it could not but dramatically engender. Christian marriage and the sanctity with which it has always been invested cannot be separated from the structure of the Christian Way.

Homosexuality is of course an ancient phenomenon. No doubt it was ill-understood by the ancients; but then it is not well understood even today. I cannot doubt, however, that the ancients were right in their instinct that it is a deviancy because it is without any purpose such as the perpetuation of the race. The ancients generally perceived it somewhat as we perceive a decadent perversion such as eating delicious food, then using an emetic to vomit it up so that one may again titillate one's taste buds all over again without stomach upset or fear of putting on weight. This perversion, less unusual in certain affluent circles than some might suppose, disgusts most of us because it so obviously bypasses the purpose of nourishment of body and soul. Eating, on a Christian view, is sacramental; hence grace before meals. It may be accompanied by the pleasures of taste, but to pervert it into a mere means of obtaining as much from our taste buds as can be squeezed out of them is revolting. So then, all forms of sexual activity, including homosexual ones, that make sexual pleasure a goal in itself are, in the view I would seek to uphold, contrary to the Christian life. Nothing that Plato says in the *Symposium* or elsewhere can, in my view, make homosexuality an acceptable alternative life style for a Christian. Deep friendships between persons of the same sex can indeed be instruments of great spiritual growth, for we learn at least as much from what is like us as from what is unlike, but sexual relationships between persons of the same sex are as destructive of that means of growth as they are of the family.

That there are special cases is obvious and was always recognized. We are grievously wrong, however, if we use them as a means of making homosexuality an acceptable life style. The mature Christian will show compassion to the victim of every imaginable kind of deviancy and perversion but will by no means condone, much less encourage it.

Christian love, then, is rooted in the same natural instincts, including the sexuality that permeates our nature, that we share with all human beings. Christians claim, however, that through their relationship with the Risen Christ they have a special means of overcoming the fetters of our human prison and reaching into a higher spiritual consciousness. Christian marriage ministers notably to the process; hence in the Marriage Service allusion is traditionally made to the comparison of Christian marriage to "the mystical union that is betwixt Christ and his Church."

Sexual attitudes that inhibit spiritual growth are to be much deplored. Yet Christians must not forget that failures to live up to the ideals delineated for those who seek to go the Christian Way are by no means the gravest or the most pernicious sins. On the contrary, they can be indeed venial compared with malice of heart, hatred of others, cruelty, and greed.

Dante recognized this when he put wanton lovers in the least horrible circle of hell. He found Francesca of Rimini there and heard the story of her having succumbed to the temptation of seizing an opportunity for sexual intercourse with her husband's more handsome brother and of their being then discovered by Lanciotto, her husband, who in a rage slew the adulterous pair. Dante was so touched that he "through compassion fainted . . . and like a corpse fell to the ground." So does the greatest of medieval poets symbolize on the one hand the danger to which sexual passion can expose us and, on the other, how slight are its effects upon the soul compared with other far deadlier sins. For wherever our moral failures are touched, be it ever so slightly, by genuine love, some effluence of that love heals the wound. Here as in so much else Dante spreads out for us the richness of the tapestry of the Christian outlook on sex and love.

GUIDELINES

Then what guidelines can we give to spiritually-minded people in today's confusing world for maintaining an ideal such as is to be found in the Christian tradition? Every priest knows from his experience in the confessional and elsewhere that for the vast majority of young people the difficulty of trying to conform to traditional Christian precepts on sex and love looms larger in many cases than anything else. Moreover, for sensitive people in love the acceptance of the old standards often presents grave problems. The gulf between the permissive sexual morality that happens to be widely fashionable in contemporary American society and what they perceive as a nobler ideal of restraint in the interest of a higher kind of interpersonal love seems so wide that many feel there ought to be some middle way, some compromise between an almost barn-yard attitude to sex on the one hand and, on the other, the demand for a standard of sexual conduct so rigid as to seem beyond human endurance. Surely, they ask, the Christian tradition needs updating for our contemporary world?

Such young people's misgivings and doubts are not only natural; they are reasonable. They call for a clear and definite answer.

The first observation to be made is that, confusing as may be the situation for anyone trying to conform to Christian models of conduct in today's world, this world is really, *in respect of the prevailing sexual mores*, not really very different from that of the Mediterranean that the Christian communities of the first few centuries had to face. Christian parents and others who sought to bring up their children to an understanding of the higher values of life had very much the same concerns then as they have now and the same problems in dealing with these concerns. Look at, say, the *Address on Vainglory and the Right Way for Parents to Bring Up Their Children* by John Chrysostom (c. 347-407). Despite an interval of some 1500 years, the situation we face parallels his in an astonishing degree. He laments, for instance, the frivolous chit-chat to which children are exposed: "Such and such a girl kissed such and such a man and had no luck and hanged herself." He deplores the fashionable young man who "wears his hair long at the back and makes himself look like a girl." He especially deplores lewd shows of "harlots, mimes, and dancers" and suggests that a good parent might usefully take a son or daughter to see the spectators at such shows emerge from the theatre and point out to them the disturbed look on the sad faces that had been watching such spectacles and how ill they compare with the happy faces of men and women who have been gathered together in the holy joy of profitable conversation and sacred study.

Chrysostom is very well aware that the attitude of the

ancient pagan world toward sexual behavior (so like that of our own) is radically opposed to that which he thinks ought to prevail in the Christian Household of Faith. He frankly admits that he knows of no easy answer. Nevertheless, he urges early training by wise Christian parents who will see that their children learn from the very first to know the value of the love of family as a means of fostering an understanding and appreciation of the joys of the spiritual life. Such training does not by any means guarantee either a trouble-free adolescence or a life of mature chastity; but it does provide a *model* that cannot ever be entirely forgotten or ignored.

He also seeks to encourage early marriage where young people from such Christian homes have fallen in love. They will strengthen each other in resistance to the follies of the world, which in the end bring only an emptiness and disappointment that he likens to a pomegranate that looks juicy and desirable but turns out to be dry and lifeless. The problem as he depicts it is very much the perennial problem of trying to live a spiritual life in the midst of a culture whose orientation is not only fundamentally alien but hostile to such a lifestyle.

The Christian standard of sexual conduct has always been seen as difficult to follow. Wise parents have recognized that even the least recalcitrant among their children would find great difficulty in reaching anything like the standard dictated by Christian tradition. Moreover, the most loving among their children would often face the worst difficulties and have the stormiest passage through life. The difference (an all-important one) that training in early years provides lies in the *ideal* by which all sexual conduct can be measured. Parents and teachers who are truly wise and mature in their spirituality will not be shocked by lapses or even deviations from the standard, so long as the ideal is kept in view. Less perceptive parents and teachers have often failed, of course, to grasp the importance of non-shockability and have succeeded in alienating their children by insisting on the realization of a standard beyond their children's capacity and strength.

We have at least one advantage that our forefathers lacked. We ought to be able to see better than they ever could that our sexual appetites and therefore the mastery of these appetites lie in the mind more than in the body. If we really want to control these appetites for the sake of an end such as the maintenance of a Christian standard of conduct and the development of a spiritual life, we shall recognize the primacy of mind and not treat our sexuality as merely a physical condition. It is the mind that governs the hormones and that can therefore direct and control our sexual life if we choose so to control it for a worthy end. First, however, we must be persuaded that the end is worth the effort, and we must also be thoroughly convinced that mind really has the primacy. We must be prepared, moreover, to go far beyond cheap strategy and tactics.

16

So get this experience of husbands and wives, and friends, and little loves; you will get through them safely if you never forget what you really are. Never forget this is only a momentary state and that we have to pass through it. Experience is the one great teacher —experience of pleasure and pain—but know it is only an experience. It leads, step by step, to that state where all things become small, and the Purusha (The Higher Self) so great that the whole universe seems as a drop in the ocean and falls off by its own nothingness.
Herbert Slade, Contemplative Intimacy

JAY G. WILLIAMS

Marriage and Sexuality in Judaism

It is best to understand this essay as a sort of fantasy, an imagined explanation of how, if I were a Jew, I might think. Although I have studied Judaism intensively, I am not Jewish and hence can hardly speak for Judaism. Rather, what I propose to do is to examine certain important passages from Hebrew Scripture and on the basis of them sketch a possible Jewish theological approach to our subject. Whether or not any Jews would agree with me, I do not know.

Truth to tell, traditional Jewish attitudes toward sexuality and marriage are not, for the most part, "spiritually" oriented. By and large, Judaism is left with a set of morals about sex but with little by way of "spiritual" interpretation. As in Christianity, the theological roots of Judaism's view of sex have either been eroded or replaced by other roots which find their inspiration in modern secularism. The Talmud provides rules, insights, and narratives about the male-female relationship. Both the *halakah* (legal opinion) and *aggadah* (narrative) rest ultimately upon faith in God; yet there is little sense in the Talmud that this is related to what might broadly be called "spirituality." It is a matter of obedience to the commandments as interpreted by the rabbis. This does not mean, however, that a spiritual view of sex could not emerge out of Judaism. There are important spiritual dimensions in the Hebrew Scriptures and traditions which can be explored and that, in this essay, is what is intended.

The relation between male and female provides, in the Hebrew Scriptures, the central metaphor for understanding both God and Israel. The narrative of the Torah is *in nuce* the story of the courtship, betrothal, and marriage of those two lovers, Yahweh (God) and Israel.[1] It is at Sinai that they affirm their vows in a prototypical marriage covenant. The prophets frequently return to this metaphor in order to explore the meaning of the demise of Israel as an independent nation; at least some of the Writings, the third part of the Hebrew canon, also allude to Israel as the bride of God and God as the lover of Israel.

Perhaps metaphor is the wrong word. For the Bible the marriage of God and Israel is the reality; it is human marriage which is a metaphor which only adumbrates true marriage. Read in one direction, at least, the story of God and Israel provides the reality according to which human marriage ought to be shaped. The covenant, then, is the key to understanding that most human of relationships: marriage.

For Plato, God spends his time "doing geometry." Truth is understood as objective, clear, and logically demonstrable. For the rabbis, God is in heaven "making marriages." Truth is what groom pledges to bride and bride to groom. The archaic nuptial phrase, "plight thee my troth," is an attempt to capture that meaning. It makes clear the radical

gulf which separates Biblical narrative and Greek philosophy. For the Bible, the paradigm for truth is not a Euclidean
demonstration of a geometrical relationship, but a faithful
couple happily celebrating its golden wedding anniversary.
In order to understand either the Bible or Judaism we must
begin with this understanding of what truth is.

Genesis, the first book of the Torah immediately makes
clear the importance of the male-female relation for the
thought-forms of ancient Israel. In Genesis 1:26 God
creates humanity in his own image and likeness, an action
which has kept interpreters busy ever since. God's image
has been variously interpreted as "the divine spark" within
humans, as personhood, as the capacity for freedom, as
humanity's triune nature (reason, will, emotion), as consciousness, as reason alone. The list is almost endless.
Genesis, itself, however, provides an unexpected meaning:

> God created man in the image of himself, in the image of
> God he created him, male and female he created them.
> (Gen. 1:27)

That is, God's image is somehow made manifest in the
fact that humans are male and female. This is the source of
human procreation; it is the means whereby humans can
fill the earth and subdue it. (Gen. 1:28) It is also a reflection
of the source of the divine ability to create. One might argue
that the world comes into being because God is a perfect
union of opposites. God is not two people who occasionally
unite. There is no separate or separable Mother Goddess.
To think of God as two is to think of an imperfect union
which is less than eternal. Hence worship of the Mother
Goddess is anathema to Biblical writers. In God, male and
female are perfectly and eternally united and because of
this, God's creation is not occasional but continuous.

Today, with our modern knowledge of biology and psychology, we might press this notion in directions only
adumbrated by the Hebrew Scriptures. We know now, for
instance, that each person is the result of a combination of
genes from both male and female. The gender of the

individual may be male or female, but there is within each person, written into the very code which provides the essential form of life, both a female and a male side. On a physical level, estrogen and testosterone are to be found in all individuals. It is their proportion which varies and creates the characteristics of gender. Chemically, the difference between male and female is one of degree.

There are also two sides to the human brain and these seem to handle functions traditionally associated with male (logic, analysis, discrimination) and female (emotion, intuition, a sense of wholeness).[2] Human consciousness and freedom, one could argue, emerge from the fact that there is interaction between what are essentially two persons within one being. The mystery of both God and man is that each is many and yet one. That God is "One" ahad is more than an assertion that God is an indivisible integer. In God, opposites exist in perfect unity and harmony.

All of this may be leading us far from the original intent of the author. Surely little was known in antiquity about genes, hormones, and bicameral brains. Still, ancient peoples were keen observers of the world and humanity. Biblical writers surely pondered the mysteries of procreation through which two became one. Myths of the ancient world regularly express the reality of what Jung has called the animus and the anima in the individual. And Genesis does, rather clearly, connect the mystery of the male-female relation with the mystery of God himself.

The second chapter of Genesis complements the first by describing in further mythic detail the creation of humanity. According to this story, Adam (humanity) was originally created one. As such Adam was whole and complete, but lonesome. "It is not good," says God, "that Adam should be alone." (Gen. 2:18) Hence, after a certain amount of experimentation which led to the creation of animals, God finally took one half of Adam and turned that half into woman.[3] As a consequence, Adam lost primal oneness in order to gain what oneness cannot provide, i.e. companionship.

The loss of that primal hermaphroditic unity was essential for human well-being, but it was also at least the
occasion, if not the cause, of a dramatic change in human
mentality. The story of the separation of male and female is
followed immediately in Genesis by the story of the "fall" of
humanity. Whether this was truly a fall or another inevitable result of the human situation is a question which can
be long debated.[4] What is certainly true is that following the
creation of male and female out of Adam, and the subsequent opening of their eyes, a world of distinctions
emerged, a world which is portrayed graphically when the
male and the female recognize their own nakedness.
Humans become corrupted by the knowledge of good and
evil and begin to judge the world according to these categories. As a result, humans become alienated from their
work, their biological roles, and from each other. The
ability to judge good and evil leaves woman dissatisfied
with the male, her supposed Lord and Master, and the
male dissatisfied with the companion whom he now blames
for having caused the problem in the first place. (Gen. 3:8-
19) This situation of alienation also reflects the human
separation from God, for the Bible sees that the marriage
bond is a direct reflection of the divine-human relationship.
Tension between male and female invariably reflects that
internal tension between the male and female elements of
the individual. The male who cannot accept the female
essentially cannot accept that hidden half of himself and, of
course, the same *mutantis mutandis* is also true of the
female. It is this internal disorder which separates humanity from God. Knowledge of God is rooted in the perfect
harmony which emerges when the sexual poles of personality cohere in mutual acceptance.

The Bible sees that the age before Noah was one in which
disorder was rampant. Sexuality was corrupted, marriage
was corrupted; and hence the divine-human relationship
was corrupted (Gen. 6:1-8). Eventually, the whole of human
society, full of violence, was destroyed by a great deluge of

primordial water. In its aftermath, God sought to establish a new and better way, the way of Israel.

Writing long after the beginning of Israel, the prophet Ezekiel describes what God did:

> The Lord Yahweh says this: By origin and birth you belong to the Land of Canaan. Your father was an Amorite and your mother a Hittite. At birth, the very day you were born, there was no one to cut your navel string, or wash you in cleansing water, or rub you with salt, or wrap you in napkins. No one leaned kindly over you to do anything like that for you. You were exposed in the open fields; you were as unloved as that on the day you were born.
> I saw you struggling in your blood as I was passing, and I said to you as you lay in your blood: Live, and grow like the grass of the fields. You developed, you grew, you reached marriageable age. Your breasts and your hair both grew, but you were quite naked. Then I saw you as I was passing. Your time had come, I bound myself by oath, I made a covenant with you—it is the Lord Yahweh who speaks—and you became mine. I bathed you in water, I washed the blood off you, I anointed you with oil. I gave you embroidered dresses, fine leather shoes, a linen headband and a cloak of silk. I loaded you with jewels, gave you bracelets for your wrists and a necklace for your throat. I gave you nose ring and earrings; I put a beautiful diadem on your head. You were loaded with gold and silver, and dressed in fine linen and embroidered silks. Your food was the finest flour, honey and oil. You grew more and more beautiful; and you rose to be queen. The fame of your beauty spread through the nations, since it was perfect, because I had clothed you with my own splendor—it is the Lord Yahweh who speaks. (Ezekiel 16:15-43)

In a word, then, God chose Israel to be his bride and in that marriage he established the basis for reunion between God and humanity, male and female. The covenant made at Sinai was the marriage of God and humanity, the ultimate union of opposites, the restoration of wholeness. To achieve this goal, Israel had only to love God with all her heart, soul, and strength.

The problem, of course, was that Israel did not, perhaps could not do this. Almost immediately Israel began to reveal a less than single-minded love of her husband. While Moses was still on the mountain, Israel turned from her husband to dance before the Golden Calf. (Ex. 32:1ff) When she entered the Promised Land, she immediately began to play the harlot, worshipping Ba'al of Peor. (Num. 25:1ff) As a result, what was meant to be the union of opposites became a new relationship of alienation governed by cultic laws. (Ex. 34:10-28)

Nevertheless, the ideal remained, an ideal to which Israel was expected to adhere. Israel was God's chosen bride. He loved her with the over-flowing *hesed* (love) which knew no bounds. Israel was called to respond with *ahavah*, a yearning, passionate love which seeks unity through complete surrender.

It was the prophets of Israel who developed most fully this metaphor of the people's marriage and subsequent unfaithfulness to God. Hosea, perhaps the most explicit of all the prophets on this point, marries a prostitute to act out God's situation in the world. Jeremiah depicts the situation as even worse, refusing to marry in order to reveal the great divorce between Israel and God which has taken place. Ezekiel, in his turn, is commanded not to mourn the death of his wife in order to reveal God's lack of grief over the fall of Jerusalem.

All the prophets see that Israel, despite God's gracious favor, has been unfaithful to her husband and, as a result, adultery and harlotry are rife in the land. Adam, like Humpty-Dumpty, is not so easily put together again. Nevertheless, no prophetic book is without some word of hope for a restoration in the future. Israel, once punished, will be taken back. The Messiah will come, a new covenant will be established.

Not all Biblical writers, however, are so sanguine. The writer of Ecclesiastes, for instance, turns from such hopes entirely to view life with a very pragmatic, if paradoxical, eye. Marriage for Ecclesiastes isn't evil—two are better than one, he says—but he has no trust in women and no sense that God's covenant with Israel provides a perspective for understanding marriage. For the writer, God is in heaven, enigmatic and largely unknowable. There is no hint of the union of opposites at all.

Still another work, the Song of Songs, provides a different answer. No one can be absolutely sure what the original intent of the author of this great poetic work really was, but it is clear that he or she took a very positive attitude toward sex. There is no asceticism or prudery here. The poem begins:

> O that you would kiss me with the kisses of your mouth!
> For your love is better than wine . . .
> (Song of Solomon 1:2)

The "plot" of this dramatic poem, however, is difficult to interpret and depends very much upon how certain key lines are translated. I believe that on the whole the Revised Standard Version makes the most sense out of the original and implies the following scenario:

The singer is a dark and comely girl who has been taken to Solomon's harem. Though he lavishes attention upon her and rehearses his romantic, if somewhat ludicrous "line," she will have none of him. Her lover is a shepherd lad whom she hopes will come to save her. In fact, she glimpses him on occasion in the city. One night she goes about the city searching for him only to be beaten by the guards for being out after hours.

The shepherd is coming but has not yet arrived. Solomon, the great king is provisionally in control and the girl can only wait with yearning for her lover, resisting to the end Solomon's overtures.[5]

> Make haste, my beloved,
> and be like a gazelle
> or a young stag
> upon the mountains of spice.
> (Song of Songs 8:14)

Many Biblical scholars resist allegorization, but in this case must admit that the poem was placed in the canon for its allegorical meaning. If our reading is correct, the allegory is clear. Israel, the girl, is confined by the opulent and tempting powers of this world, in the harem of Solomon. It would be all too easy to succumb to the blandishments of the world. But she still yearns for her true lover, God, who somehow, some way, will come to save her from her plight. Some day, they will run away to the desert and be united once more. Until that time, Israel must resist the temptations of the flesh and remain pure and holy.

If this reading is correct, it expresses very well the mood of much post-exilic Judaism. Its message is anything but uninhibited sensuality. Rather the Song of Songs teaches Israel to shun the world and hope in the return of God. Seen in this light, the poem may be the most Messianic book in Scripture. A Messianic view of sexuality is implied which we must not overlook. Sex is good, if the lover is right, but one must beware the misdirected desires of the flesh, for they will only ensnare and make the individual a captive in the world of sensation. Israel must wait and hope in the God who will return to restore the covenant and reestablish the union of opposites once more. The ultimate fulfillment of desire is God himself.

As the post-exilic era wore on without any clear moment of restoration or reconciliation, Judaism's mood clearly changed. Ancient Israel, despite its elaborate legal codes, did very little to legislate about sexual questions. There were some rules concerning such matters as bestiality, sodomy, and incest, but the Torah is hardly explicit about a whole range of issues including divorce and polygamy. By and large, pre-exilic Israel depended upon common tradition rather than legal code for regulating sexual relations. Therefore, it would be difficult to establish a full sexual ethic based upon the Torah alone. Clearly, ancient Israelites, though by no means hedonists, were not particularly prudish about sexual questions either.

In the post-exilic, second Commonwealth period, this

free and easy attitude was to change drastically as the Rabbis sought to work out a complex legal system designed to cover all aspects of life. Louis M. Epstein writes,

> The standards of sex morality were radically changed during the Second Commonwealth. The naivete and innocence which characterized the old period yielded to worldly suspicion. This worldliness was the result of the new setting in which the post-exilic Jew found himself, commerce to a large extent replacing agriculture, city life succeeding narrow rural existence. The worldliness of the broader civilization quite naturally begot a sense of uncertainty, culminating in pessimism, and from pessimism there is but one step to asceticism. Uncertainty also has the opposite effect, that of tightening inner bonds, drawing in one's sails, so to speak, resulting in rigorous discipline and legalism. These four, worldliness, pessimism, asceticism, and legalism, had their combined bearing on the sex of the day.[6]

We might wish to take issue with the author concerning the naivete of pre-exilic Israel and concerning the causes for the growing pessimism, but his central point is certainly well taken: Judaism became very suspicious of sexuality outside the strict bonds of marriage and came to hedge in the practice of Jews by a corpus of legal opinions. The *yezer hara*, largely to be identified with the sexual impulse, became something to be mistrusted and feared.

Never, however, did this pessimism and asceticism become complete. God at the very beginning commanded humans to be fruitful and multiply and that imperative could not be circumvented. The *mikveh* had to be fulfilled. Indeed, it was common belief that no human was complete outside the bonds of marriage. An unmarried adult was considered virtually immoral, for God's primal commandment was not being taken seriously.

Moreover, as time went on the pessimism and ascetic views of the Hellenistic world faded somewhat. The compilers of the Talmud, though still sometimes suspicious of sexuality, took, on the whole, a reasonable and balanced view. Marriage was highly praised and the sexual urge itself accepted as blessed by God, if expressed within acceptable bounds. The role of women was defended against the tendency to confinement and virtual enslavement. There are important attempts in the Talmud to protect the widow and other women in difficulty not of their own making.

In the Talmud, however, the spiritual position hinted at in Scripture remains undeveloped. The Talmud tends to emphasize legal cases rather than metaphysics. Relations between the sexes were taken in a straightforward, moral way. It was left to the esoteric Kabbalists to pick up and develop the more esoteric features of ancient Scripture.[7]

For the Kabbala, the physical world, like the spiritual world, is a manifestation of God and hence is essentially good. This means that sex is good, its urging, the command of God. Moreover—and here the Kabbalists seem to have sensed what Scripture hints at—God himself is bound together with love. There is an essential attraction, metaphorically described as sexual, between God and his Shekinah or Spirit. In true worship, their unity is fulfilled and God's Oneness can be proclaimed. The congregation of Israel is, as it were, lifted up into the Godhead as the Shekinah rises, in prayer and praise, to unite in God. From a human point of view, this is experienced as religious ecstasy. From a divine point of view, the union of God and his Shekinah is the fulfillment of the Godhead, the unity which is the source of all creation and the truth which is heralded in the great Shemah:

Hear, O Israel, the Lord your God is one. (Deut. 6:4)

In the modern world, however, in the face of rational, scientific thought, the influence of the Kabbala has declined severely. Nevertheless, the potential for a spiritual view of sex can still be found in Judaism. As we review the basic themes of Hebrew Scriptures and traditions it would seem that a Jewish approach to the question might well develop along the following lines:

1. The relation between male and female both among and within individuals reflects something of the mystery of God himself. To become one with your own internal sexual opposite is to know something of the mystery of God's oneness. The relation between male and female reveals to us the very nature of God.

2. To become reconciled and harmonized with someone of the opposite sex, one must first come to terms with the realities of that sex within. A man cannot truly love a woman without accepting and loving himself as woman. The same is true also, of course, of the woman. In a curious sense, one can only love another insofar as one loves oneself.

3. This reconciliation, however, is not easy. We have eaten of the tree of knowledge of good and evil and therefore find ourselves strangely alienated from ourselves and our world. We suppress and reject our own duality and as a consequence we reject both our sexual opposite and God himself. The history of Israel witnesses to the great difficulty humans have in becoming reconciled to the realities of their own nature.

4. There are moments of miracle when male and female form a perfect union. These ecstatic moments offer a hint of the Messianic kingdom which is to come, for when the time is fulfilled, God's oneness will be perfectly reflected in each individual.

5. The binding force of God's Oneness is love, which in Hebrew is of two types. God's love for Israel is called *hesed* and is an out-pouring, bountiful, enduring love. Israel's love for God is *ahavah*, a yearning, devoted, self-giving love. The oneness of the personality is characterized by the intermeshing of these two mutually accepting loves. The erotic is by no means excluded but is taken up into a love which accepts rather than simply uses.

6. When this circle of love is manifest in the individual another can then be brought into the circle. Self-acceptance by male or female issues in love of the opposite

sex. Marriage is the manifestation of the cosmic cycle of love which binds God together.

The effects of love are not confined to marriage. Violence, crime, war, hatred are all, at root, manifestations of the inability to accept all aspects of the self. When the self is bound together in reciprocal love, then violence itself is destroyed. Violence cannot exist in the face of self-acceptance.

7. In this life, however, our self-acceptance is bound to be imperfect. There are always areas of the self which remain unaccepted. Then hate emerges and the world turns violent. We have become corrupted by the knowledge of good and evil and because of this cannot return to cosmic unity. But we need not be lost in despair. Intimations of divine love are there. Although we remain shut up in the worldly seraglio of Solomon, the shepherd lad passes close by our door. In due time, he will come to fulfill in us the promise of his image.

Marriage, on the one hand, is seen by the Hebraic tradition with sober and open eyes. Two imperfect creatures are bound to know hate as well as moments of love. Sometimes separation and/or divorce is necessary. There must be laws to preserve both the frail institution of marriage and protect the individual from a relation of hate which sometimes develops.

Nevertheless, marriage is also a spiritual estate in which divinely unifying love can be known. It is a glimpse of heavenly ecstasy, a fulfillment of humanity's deepest spiritual needs. Marriage is not *just* a pragmatic union for the purpose of bearing and raising children. It must be treasured as the fountainhead of our deepest spirituality. It is the reconstitution of the Primal Man known in the Bible as Adam.

REFERENCES

1. Jay G. Williams, *Ten Words of Freedom* (Philadelphia: Fortress Press, 1971), pp. 88-92.

2. Such associations are, of course, caricatures. Many women are highly logical; many men, very emotional. Nevertheless, recent studies show that there are, in fact, mental as well as physical differences between men and women. These differences tend to follow the lines established by our "folk wisdom."

3. The word *sayla*, usually translated "rib" in Genesis 2, can be, and it would seem more logically should be, translated "side." This is the only place in Scripture where *sayla* is interpreted to be a human rib.

4. Jay G. Williams, "Genesis 3," *Interpretation*, Vol XXXV, No. 2, July 1981.

5. Jay G. Williams, *Understanding the Old Testament* (New York: Barron's, 1972), pp. 295-97.

6. Louis M. Epstein, *Sex Laws and Customs in Judaism* (New York: KTav Publishing, 1967), pp. 5-6.

7. Jay G. Williams, *Judaism* (Wheaton, Ill.: Theosophical Publishing House, 1980), pp. 89-93.

17

When you make the two one, and when you make the inner as the outer and the outer as the inner and the above as the below, and when you make the male and the female into a single one, so that the male will not be male and the female [not] be female . . . then shall you enter the Kingdom.

The Gospel according to Thomas

SRI M. P. PANDIT

The Spiritual Dimension of the Sexual Revolution

May He forever protect us
May we enjoy our labors
May our study become luminous
May we never hate
Peace, Peace, Peace

Sex is one subject around which many taboos have gathered over the years. Almost every religion associates sex with sin. Is there really original sin as they say?

Sri Aurobindo, my teacher, would say there is no sin except ignorance. Ignorance here means not knowing oneself and one's relation to reality; the ignorance of thinking about division between oneself and others is a sin. The fall of man is the fall from the sense of oneness into a sense of separativeness. The more one grows in consciousness, in knowledge, the more the ignorance recedes. Ignorance has to recede as knowledge grows.

Almost all religious traditions of the past, and therefore social traditions of the world that have been bathed in the religions, say that sex is sinful. The pleasure associated with sex is considered to be sensual and an obstacle to reaching God. Why? For centuries and centuries, both in the East and the West this misapprehension has continued. Recently though, the spirit of man, his nature, has revolted as it revolted against the wrong ideas and conceptions of God. Now it has revolted against wrong ideas of sex. Sex is being made a legitimate part of life. It now has a role.

An objective view of things would show that money, power, and sex are three great forces in the present constitution of the human universe. Every person is naturally attracted to money, force, power, aggrandizing with power of any kind, and sex—these are universal forces, they are not contributions of any individual.

Sex is a universal force in nature. Nature has endowed so much with force, or sex, in order to effectuate her own intention of the perpetuation of the species. If the drive behind sex were not intense, if the pleasure principle were not sharp, few would bother to procreate and become involved with the consequent responsibilities.

Since sex is a universal force that will prevail upon whoever is ready, it will awaken in that one through desire. It is through desire that a man and a woman come together. They are attracted to each other, though without an effectual basis, purely out of some affinity; then nature steps in and creates desire and lust. She watches to see if the man and woman can be precipitated into fulfilling her purpose. So where is sin? If there is sin, it is the sin of nature and not of us as individuals. It is like hunger—we don't blame ourselves if we are hungry.

Deeper than all this there is another principle, one perceived and consecrated into spiritual truths by the tradition of the *tantras*, which is the underlying principle of this universe. After all changes are eliminated from the manifested world, something remains, and that is the spirit. We

call it the Absolute. Now this Absolute is beyond definition, beyond description. It is the Absolute Reality. Though
it cannot be known by the mind, though it cannot be expressed by human speech, it reveals itself to human consciousness in three terms. It reveals itself as sheer "existence," or *sat*. The nature of this existence, or sat, is "consciousness," or *chit*—something self-aware and all-aware.
The character of this conscious being is "delight," or
ananda. So you have sat, chit, and ananda. It is out of an
ebullition of delight that this universe comes to be. To manifest this delight in every particle, in every atom is the
intention.

We are all involved in an evolutionary moment that
places us at a mid-stage. That is why we do not see the
pervading principle of delight, but there is in us, underlying
all of our day-to-day experience, something delightful—
emotions, mental serenity, and at the physical and vital
levels, sex. In one sense, sex is the channel through which
the human individual relates himself, or offers himself to
the flow of delight.

In spiritual disciplines, practiced in their purity centuries
ago, sex was utilized as a way to open up the clogged nerve
channels that stand between man and God. Then sex is part
of spiritual discipline. But this is so only when one com-
mingles one's spirit with another, where there is no passion,
when one loses one's sense of individuality and offers the
fruit to the divine. Many Western writers and speakers on
the tantras conveniently forget to point out that sex and the
tantra have got to be free from desire, free from passion.

The tantra makes three categories of practitioners. First
is the crude man, the slave of desire, he who is driven by
passion and is called the animal man; he has no right to
practice sex as part of the tantra. Second, there is the hero
man who has risen above passion, above desires, above
inertia, who is dynamic, is a channel for the flow of joy to
the divine. And third, there is the God-man, the man who is
above. He does not care for sex, sex has no relevance to
him. Sex to him is part of a spiritual effort to embrace

everything in life and turn it toward God, to utilize every experience in life for the ascension of consciousness toward God. This type of sex was not prohibited, it was not enjoined. It was clearly said that those whose natures are so made can participate in sex without the animal passions. For them, tantra was permissible, and their emotions were enhanced by it.

It is very easy to deceive ourselves into saying that we have no desire, we have no passion. When this movement grew there was great impurity, there was great self-deception, and the tantra collectively ceased to be practiced in India from that time. In India we do not practice tantra, we do not hear much of tantra; it is only when I come to the West that I see all these groups and people speaking of tantra and asking me questions about kundalini and sex. Nobody practices kundalini in India. It has no relevance. That laborious process has no meaning at the close of the twentieth century. Human consciousness has grown so much, there has been such an explosion of knowledge that all those old primitive methods are not necessary; but, tantras today have been aligned to sex. Many people speak of tantra only as a way to salve their guilty conscience.

I admit that there is no question of conscience in sex. Western seekers ask me, "Is it wrong for a spiritual teacher to have sex with his disciple?" There is no spiritual discipline in the world that requires the guru, or teacher to have sex relations with his disciple. Neither transmission of energy nor grace requires this crude exchange. If you're honest, have it as a man and a woman, but not as a guru and a disciple. These things should not be confused.

Then what is the role of sex? I made it clear that there is no sin attached to sex. Sex is a biological function, it is a device of nature at all levels of nature. The freeing of sex today is an understandable revolt against the taboos and blind prejudices that have grown around sex. It is nature's way of clearing the path to bring about this reaction. It is inevitable that when there is a reaction there are abuses. There are in every such mass movement. We speak of the

French Revolution, the Bolshevik Revolution, all kinds of political revolution. Every one may bring about some desired end, but it is attended by great violence, a lot of injustice; similarly, this shaking off of the old barriers and taboos about sex by the present generation is an understandable and perhaps a desirable moment of explosion, which will clear the way for further human evolution.

Once the mystery about sex and the hiding of it are removed, the obviousness of sex makes it less enchanting. You may have heard how, in Denmark, which was the one country in Europe where the pornographic movement was most intense, the majority of the establishments closed because there was no interest in sex pornography anymore. The only people who would visit would be tourists. Sex lost its attraction in that form.

It is therefore a device of nature to open up the topic of sex. Once the glamor of the forbidden is seen, all the glamor is removed. Naturally, in the process of clearing, there are abuses. Normal sex becomes boring. Other forms take place and these too will become boring. Human nature is such that it cannot stick to one form of entertainment or pleasure for very long. It will try to invent something else, and the human brain is very fertile in this matter.

But this is a transitional passage, because sex pertains only to a certain state in the development of humanity. As long as we live mostly in the physical, in the vital domain, the domain of physical pleasure and vital excitement, sex attracts, but once we move in consciousness beyond the physical, sex becomes irrelevant. When one's consciousness is centered around a light turning upwards, expanding in cosmic dimensions, sex is absolutely irrelevant. This is in line with the vision of the occultists that sex as a means of procreation will cease to play a part in the future. As the new consciousness, the new age for which we are confidently preparing emerges, sex will lose its power and hold over human beings.

We have about two thousand people living in our community, and we have a center of education where there are about seven hundred students. One of the girls of the school once asked my teacher, the Mother, "Is it true that women are inferior to men?" The Mother said "That has interested me greatly. I also have been told that women are inferior and in many of the religious traditions, women have no right to participate in certain rituals, things are kept back from them. So," she said "I wanted to find out what the truth is behind this differentiation of sex." Once, during her meditation, she released herself from the physical body and went straight to the Source of creation to see what the truth was behind the sex differentiation. There she found that this distinction did not exist at all. On the other hand, male and female denote, on the higher planes of existence, a presiding voice of consciousness. The female represents the executor, the dynamic part of consciousness, something to support and preside, something to execute and dynamize. It is only as creation comes "lower" and "lower" that this sex differentiation in the physical body starts for purposes of nature; but that age is ending.

It is a confirmed perception, and to a certain extent a viable experience, that as individuals develop spiritually, as the higher consciousness replaces the normal human consciousness, the sex organs of the body undergo change. Sex as a process of procreation has become impermanent.

Today one reproduces oneself in a physical manner through sex. The mental man, the great writer, the one who has a vision, reproduces himself at the mental level, through his expression of writing. A transformed man, a gnostic man, a divinized man reproduces himself in a divinized way, not through sex. This is the future toward which we are going; a future where sex will not play any role. As man evolves, sex will play a lesser role. This may happen one thousand, perhaps five thousand years later; we do not know, as this time factor is not forseeable. That is the direction in which human evolution is going, and what is happening today is just as well. It makes sex so obvious that it loses attraction. The real sexual revolution is not where you dissipate sex energies, but where you insist on conserving sex energy.

Yogic science has a very rational explanation of the necessity of conserving sex energy. Sex energy is one of the expressions of the inherent energy of the human body; highly creative, highly powerful. As the body develops, it comes to a certain stage of being full of sex energy. Nature exerts herself through desire, through passions, through lust to draw out the energy and use it for her purposes of continuing the species. However, if a responsible person, an awakened person preserves that energy instead of throwing it out, it gathers heat in the body and, like water becoming warm and hot, it creates what is called *tapas*. Tapas is heat. As a result of this heat in the body, the will power becomes more dynamic. When this heat is cherished, preserved, allowed to grow, it turns into light. Tapas turns into *tejas*, and the result is that the brain cells get illumined; the capacity of the brain gets enhanced. The third stage is when both the heat and the light turn into a kind of inner electricity, as a result of which both the illumined brain and the dynamic will power gather. The fourth stage is when this inner electricity turns into the creative power of the primal ether, which is called *ojas*. One develops this creative ability, not necessarily in a physical way, but through thought; through will, one can create. The final consummation is that this inner energy becomes spiritual energy; not vital energy, not physical energy or mental energy, but spiritual energy, which leads to self-realization. This is the real sex revolution that human beings are called upon to bring about once they are awakened. What we are seeing now is a revolution from the other end. Both are revolutions in the sense that they seek a departure from the beaten track.

These are some of the implications of the sex revolution. I would like to sum up the main points that I have offered. Sex is not sin; sex is a legitimate part of man. Sex is relevant as long as one feels attracted to it, but, as one develops in consciousness, sex becomes irrelevant and one goes beyond. Sex experience is only a transitional experience; when it is universalized in its availability it will lose its pull. From that point of view, it is a necessary part of the evolution that we are passing through at the present moment in perhaps ugly forms of sex practices and an interest in sex that is almost a perversion of sex. Sex is considered in a spiritual context to be something holy, something sacred, and even yogic; it is only a physical expression of a real moment of love and mutual self-giving. Physical sex adds a certain physical completeness to that experience, and in doing so it awakens the doors of the emotional being to psychic delight. It is possible to use sex in its purity when it is not a result of passion but an expression of true love; in this interchange and commingling it opens the doors of the soul. There are many "ifs," and one must have purified oneself at all levels of one's being before this ascent of consciousness becomes possible.

18

He who binds to himself a joy
Doth the winged life destroy;
He who kisses the joy as it flies
Lives in Eternity's sunrise.
        William Blake

HAZRAT INAYAT KHAN

Passion

When one considers the nature of passion, one sees that it is life itself; it is energy taking substantial form and expressing itself through different channels and outlets. Different desires such as speaking, singing, dancing, laughing, crying, fighting, wrestling, boxing, are different expressions of the same energy, whose central or final expression takes place in the passion between the sexes.

Passion is seen in the groups made by speaker and listener, or thinker and receiver, or actor and spectator, but it appears most vital and strong in the love of the lover and the response of the beloved. The passion of the poet is in his poetry; the passion of the musician composes melody; the passion of the actor declaims his part. The act of creation, in no matter what aspect, is the play of passion, whose source and root is love alone; for as man without humanity is empty, and as the body without spirit is dead, so passion without love is energy that is devoid of beauty and blind.

Passion is the desire of love. Passion is the expression of love and it is the satisfaction of love. It is no exaggeration to say that passion is the end of love; for the purpose of love is fulfilled by passion. Man's life is composed of many lives, and the circle of each is completed when the passion that inspires each is satisfied.

All things in life have a purpose; the purpose of some is known, and of others unknown. And beyond life and beneath life exists that activity which the limited mind cannot comprehend. But so far as human understanding can probe, it can discover nothing of greater purpose and value to the world than passion. Under that covering is hidden the hand of the creator.

In all aspects of life, through the animal kingdom to humanity, it is the only source and cause of generation; and that of itself discloses to the thinker its importance. The great teachers of humanity have therefore wished man to look upon every expression of passion as sacred; and as most sacred of all that passion which exists in the love of the sexes for each other. The desire to make sex passion a most sacred thing is seen in the teaching of Shiva; and the origin of phallic worship lay in the desire to raise in the sight of humanity the sacredness of passion, and to free it from the shame and contempt with which men viewed it.

The desire of the ear to hear clearly shows itself when one is unable to listen owing to a disturbing noise. Then the passion of hearing is not satisfied and man becomes confused; he will beg others to keep quiet a moment, or if weak he will lose his temper if he is not allowed to listen to what he wishes to hear at the moment. When one smells a thing there comes a desire to smell it until one knows what it is, until one can fully understand and appreciate the smell. And so also with taste; the taste of a delicious dish tempts man at once to taste more, to enjoy it fully.

The sight of beauty gives man desire to see into its depths, until his sight is satisfied. In the average man the passion of touch is, however, the most intense form of sense; for through this sense consciousness comes to the surface. The comfort of soft clothing, of easy chairs, of warmth in winter, of coolness in summer, of the freshness of the bath, is conveyed to a man through his sense of touch. Indeed, most of his pleasures are dependent upon it, and this sense reaches its culmination in the passion of the body for one of the opposite sex. But it is not only the sense of touch that is energized to its very centre in sex passion; every sense is then awake, and therefore it is that sex passion moves mankind more than anything else in the world.

In each different aspect of joy a different plane of existence is reached, but in sex passion all planes of existence are in motion. When accumulated energy is expressed in the abstract through feeling, it comes as laughter or tears, anger, affection, fear, or sympathy. Energy expressed through the mind comes as speech or thought; and expressed through the body as action. But the expression of intense affection towards the opposite sex brings the whole being to the surface. Consciousness which in other experiences becomes but partially external, remaining mostly within, is brought entirely to the surface by sex passion alone. It is because of this that spiritually-minded people have abstained from sex passion and religious people have considered it degrading. For the soul-consciousness is thus brought outside instead of being preserved within, and the soul is thus brought to earth although its destination is, so to speak, heaven.

But if this world is the work of a Creator, it has been created so that He might experience external life. In other words the knowing aspect of life has wished to know the knowable part of life; and its joy depended upon knowing, which alone comes through experience. Moreover its evolution and development depend on the inspiration which is brought by experience alone. And inasmuch as it is necessary for the knowing aspect of life, or the soul, to return at length to its original state of being, even so it is necessary for it to experience first of all the life it created for the very reason that it might know.

19

He who being a man,
Cherishes his feminine side,
Is in himself
A womb to the World.
He is a universal channel
Of eternal truth
Living in eternal truth
He will maintain eternal youth.
                    Kalid A. Rah, The High Way:
                        Reflections on the Tao

HERBERT GUENTHER

Male-Female Polarity in Oriental Thought

In China, the male-female polarity is represented by the fundamental forces of Yin (female) and Yang (male). The philosophical use of these terms is found in the fifth chapter of the fifth appendix of the *I Ching*, where the statement runs: "One Yin and One Yang, that is the Tao." In the further explanation by early Chinese authors, the Yin and Yang components never became fully separated, but at each stage only one is manifested and dominant, while the other is latent and recessive. Throughout the discussions of the wave-like operations of these forces there is no undertone of good and evil.[1]

While in China the attainment and maintenance of the balance between the Yin and the Yang was considered to be

---

1. Joseph Needham, *Science and Civilization in China*, vol. 2, p. 277.

the source of happiness, health, and harmony, in Japan the polarity is seen more as a tension and as playing a role. The polarity is here represented by Amaterasu, the sun-goddess, and Susanoo, the storm-god. Their relationship was, according to legend, strained, but again there is no evaluation in terms of good and evil. The female aspect was adopted as a guiding principle by the nobility, the male aspect by the warrior class, and Buddhism participated in this polarity, Kannon and Amida, both of them showing tender features, on the side of the female end of the spectrum, Fudō and Dainichi, stern and harsh, on the male end.[2]

Underlying the whole of Indian thinking is one fundamental idea which, although it has undergone various interpretations throughout the centuries and sometimes has temporarily receded into the background, has always been present. This idea is that the principles of maleness and femaleness embodied in men and women are intrinsically positive and divine in their own rights and that their implementation in male-female relationships including sex is the manifestation of the Divine so that man partakes in the divine play not only as a mere creature but as a creator himself. The *Brhadāranyaka-upanishad* elaborates this theme in a lengthy discussion, of which the following are the essential points:

> In the beginning, this (i.e. the universe) was the Virāj alone in the shape of a person . . .[3]

> He became the size of a man and woman in close embrace. He divided this body into two. From that (division) came husband (*pati*) and wife (*patni*). He united with her. From the (union) human beings were born.[4]

> He (Virāj) realized: "Indeed, I am the creation for I produced all this." Therefore He became the creator. He

---

2. Shinko Mochizuki et al., *Teihon Butsu-zō: Kokoro to Katachi*, p. 226.

3. *Brhadāranyaka-upanishad*, I IV 1.

4. *Brhadāranyaka-upanishad*, I IV 3.

who knows this becomes a creator in the creation of the Virāj.[5]

The Virāj, "The Shining One," subsequently identified with the Absolute in its comprehensible form of Ātman or Self and in personalistic terms called *purusa* "person," has within it the polarity of maleness and femaleness which is the "splendour" of reality and when it breaks up (*pat*) retains in each of its parts the splendour of its origin. There is no overevaluation of the one against the other, and the sexual union is a divine manifestation bringing about the divine nature of all that is. The whole universe thus "embodies" the divine and creative energy, and man in the copulative act re-enacts on a limited scale which is in no way less sublime, the cosmic process of creation. Maleness and femaleness as divine qualities of equal value have found artistic expression in Śiva as Ārdhanārīśvara "Half-Woman-Half Man." However, Śiva is not only the great lover, he is also the great ascetic. It is in the interpretation of this latter aspect that one of the worst cross-cultural confusions has arisen. We, in the West, have come to understand asceticism as a disparagement of everything pleasant and natural to man which was supposed to be under the wrathful ban of God, an idea that rapidly spread throughout Christianity. Indian "asceticism" has nothing to do with such an idea. The Indian word *tapas* means an accumulation of vital energy and it was practised for gaining power, for being able to accomplish tremendous works. From earliest time onwards the spiritual significance of sexuality was insisted upon and the identification of spiritual vitality and semen is still widespread today. Loss of semen, either by intercourse or spontaneous emission, is viewed with dread, because it is felt to be a loss of power. Hence, to store up this vital energy until the body is filled with it at high pressure, is not to take a dim view of sexuality, rather it is the opposite; Śiva is also known as *ūrdhvalinga* referring to the state of highest tension which is represented

---

5. *Brhadāranyaka-upanishad*, I IV 5.

in the erotic sculpture of India by his erect member. The well-known squeamishness about sex of Gandhi and the modern "export" Swamis merely reflects the unresolved conflict between Indian tradition and Victorian morality, the former more or less disowned the latter imitated and hence deceptive and deceitful.

Still, according to legend, Śiva burns Kāma, the god of love. This, too, does not imply any contempt for the emotion of love or the person arousing this emotion. On the contrary, in the same way as, in physical terms, the storing of the semen is said to lead to a heightened state of vitality, so the elimination of ego-centredness and possessiveness leads to the "abiding emotion" (sthāyibhāva) of love (śrngāra). Kāma is an "irritation," indicating a need for love, śrngāra is an abiding emotion, self-forgetful, egoless, not needing. In its experience the "lover" is one with the "beloved," not numerically, but in the sense that such terms as unity and duality no longer apply. Not only does Śiva as the great lover practise sexual intercourse for aeons, his orgasm lasts just as long. Śiva, the ascetic, and Śiva, the lover, are not so contradictory as they may seem at first glance. The symbol of Śiva-Pārvatī is the visible form of our experience when there is a total commitment of body and mind, fused in action, as it were, and giving the feeling of fulfillment.

Hinduistic Tantrism has as its philosophical basis the dualism of the Samkhya system, which, again philosophically speaking, approaches a kind of dominance psychology inasmuch as it is at the bidding of the purusa (the male element) that the prakṛti (the female element), comprising all that which we divide into matter and mind, ceases to perform her dance of evolution. Still, this dualism does not contain any evaluation in terms of good and evil. The puruṣa is conceived as light (prakāśa), radiating forth existential energy, and the prakṛti is conceived as the reflection working out of this impulse. This working out is her power or śakti and as śakti she is referred to as the consort of the purusa, usually conceived of as Śiva. In religious terms, *puruṣa is the god* Śiva, and *prakṛti* is the goddess (*devī*), and their relationship is visualized in the image of a loving couple. Since She represents the active (powerful, *śakti*) part She is usually represented as on top of Śiva lying prostrate. Moreover, the creative and revelatory role of *prakṛti* was seen in the warm and vital, personal form of a goddess, and the various aspects and stages of her creative personality were again depicted in images of goddesses. Correspondingly, in the Tantric ritual a woman was honoured and worshipped as a goddess. This was not a sentimental deification, rather the goddess was present in the earthly woman.

The Vaiṣṇava conception comes closest to the Western distinction between "sacred love" and "profane love" in the image of Kṛṣṇa and Radha and the Gopis. The great strength of the Kṛṣṇa cult has been its truly all-embracing eroticism and the exploitation of all possible minutiae of physical passion. Indian scholasticism was at pains to see in the frank eroticism an allegory of the relationship of humanity to God, but it did not condemn the sensuality involved.[6]

Philosophical Hinduism is no exception to the general idea that the female principle is intrinsically positive. Māyā, whatever its relationshiip to Brahman may be, is not itself evil. As the creative power of Brahman, Māyā is limiting, and every limitation is restrictive and biased. Cognitively speaking, Māyā is insufficient knowledge. "Good" and its correlative "evil" are judgments based on insufficient knowledge and have no abiding nature in themselves. . . .

Buddhism added a new dimension to Indian thought. Its early phase centered around the ideal of the monk, whose celibacy continued the older trend of the storage of energy, but with a different content. It was no longer a question of

---

6. Contrast with this attitude the modern Western Krishna cult which under the influences of Victorianized Hinduism adopts an extremely negative and puritanical outlook and which is utterly devoid of the warm and humanistic feeling that permeated the original version.

power but of an overwhelming experience, Nirvana, in which the polarities had been overcome. The difference between the Hindu *tapasvin* and the Buddhist monk can be stated as follows: the *tapasvin* aims at a state of highest tension, the monk at a state of tension resolved, or, at least, suspended, and while tension is closely associated with sexuality, the resolution of tension is not tied to any sex. On the other hand, the *tapasvin* and the monk are alike in their inveiglement against woman as the temptress, which is merely a comment on their personal feeling of weakness, but does not reflect a metaphysical judgment and its imposition on others for the sake of a merely hypothetical doctrine.

Male-female polarity becomes one of the central topics in Vajrayana Buddhism which emphasizes the "existential" aspect as against epistemological discussions. Its language "embodies" experience and meaning felt to be valuable and important and which are experienced both in ideas and in action. To ideas in particular, belongs the polarity of *prajnā and upāya*, to action the situation referred to by the terms Karmamudrā and Jñānamudrā. Throughout Buddhist philosophy, *prajñā* is the term for a discriminating, appreciative function, a value-cognition, while *upāya* refers to the "enactment" of what is gained through this value-cognition. The two are mutually enhancing: so much value-cognition, so much meaningful action; so much meaningful action, so much insight into reality. And since "knowledge" is the keynote, subjective opinion is automatically excluded. However, does femininity literally belong to *prajñā* or do we only fancy or imagine that it does because the noun *prajñā* is of feminine gender? The answer is that femininity literally belongs to *prajñā*. Through the awareness of our own states and including them, we are aware of things other than our own states and in this experience we are aware of femininity as invading, pervading, inherent, and indwelling in the whole texture of the function of awareness. Similarly, *upāya* involves masculinity. In more specific terms *upāya* is *karunā* "compassion," which is an active principle, not a passive sentimentality. The noun *karunā* is of feminine gender but its operation is felt as masculine. Hence the gender of the noun has no bearing on the life-process. The polarity of *prajñā* and *upayā* and their unity in the existential reality of man is described as follows by Anangavajra:

> The unreality of the entities of existence (as entities in themselves) which is arrived at by a process of discerning thought, by the division into knowledge and the knowable, is called the intention of prajñā.[7]

Here it is quite clearly stated that the nature of the entities of reality, their *nihsvabhava* or *śūnyatā* is "intended" by *prajñā*. The verse does not say that *prajñā* is *śūnyatā*; however, in order to be able to appreciate *śūnyatā*, that is, the open dimension of being, it must be "open," not biased.[8] The *prajñā* is always a function, *never* an ontological entity. Anangavajra, then, goes on to say about *upayā*:

> Compassion (*kr̥pa*) is called the passion of love (*rāga*), because it has an affection for all sentient beings that are drowning in the ocean of misery, that has arisen from the cause-factor of frustration. It is praised as meaningful action (*upāya*) because of its taking an appropriate course, just as a boat, following the current, leads to the desired destination.[9]

Anangavajra sums up the unity of this polarity in the words:

> The fusion of these two principles, like a mixture of milk and water, is called *prajñopāya* in view of their unity.[10]

The polarity of "appreciative discrimination" and "meaningful action," in philosophical terms, of "male" and

---

7. Prajñopāyaviniścayasiddhi, I 14.

8. There is a tremendous logical difference between saying that *prajñā* is *śūnya* ("open, unbiased") and stating that *prajñā* is *śūnyatā* ("an open dimension"). Unfortunately, this distinction is not always noted by Western writers.

9. *Prajñopāyaviścayassiddhi*, I 15-16; note here the social implication of "all beings."

10. Ibid., I 17.

"female" in worldly and poetic form, expresses the fundamental tendencies of humanity. There is perpetual movement, a continuous change of states, and at the same time, a
constant removal of contraries by states of relative
equilibrium. Human reality is just this state of suspended
tension between maleness and femaleness, in which both
are "open," nothing as such, and only their incessant interaction, their becoming, is real.

Human reality thus becomes a field of limitless possibilities. Man is not thrown into an alien world, he is the world,
forever creating it and in creating it creating himself. The
consequence of such a view is that man does not deal with
"objects," but with "realities," and these realities appear to
him as an embodied being as "embodiments" of creativity,
primarily in human shapes of men and women—who nevertheless remain linked to the non-human world with all its
beauty and values. These embodiments are the so-called
"deities" in whom man encounters and sees himself, and
in this encounter he learns to be more himself. It is unfortunate that we have to use personalistic terms, as they
are misleading. To be more oneself does not mean an
aggrandisement of the ego; an ego-centred person is the
last person to be himself for the simple reason that he is
unable to accept himself and consequently tries desperately
to be something other than himself. There also cannot be
any categorical division between the "human" and the
"divine"; such a division would be self-defeating and take
the life out of the real which we have seen is the tension
between contraries. It is through the "divine" symbols of
polarity that man may understand himself as a "field," in
the technical language of Buddhism called a maṇḍala. In
this "field" the male polarity is as important as the female
one, the one cannot be without the other, both are "formu-
lated energies" of knowledge which is already presupposed
in the question whether man can know and be himself. To
restrict or to denigrate knowledge is tantamount to des-
troying man's humanity. But Knowledge operates in many
ways, and each way may embody itself in a particular

symbolic form. When we said that insight into reality corresponds to meaningful action and vice versa, we find this explicitly stated in Buddhism:

> That great (i.e. absolute) knowledge that by itself is most effective in the realization of the aims of all beings, and cannot be fettered, is called Amoghasiddhi.[11]

and

> That knowledge that by means of absolute compassion always strives to retrieve the world is called Tārā because of its skill in saving the beings.[12]

Or, another example that will point to the double character of knowledge as being the most intimate "possession" a man can have and yet being most "public" because of its being connected with the rest of mankind and with the natural world:

> Jewels like a Buddha and so on, come forth of a certainty and steadily; this knowledge connected with the aspirations of the beings is called Ratnasambhava.[13]

and

> Since the knowledge (embodying) all Buddhahood is my innermost being and my own it is known as Māmakī because of mutual interpenetration.[14]

As long as there are human beings, the male-female polarity will continue. This polarity is not mutually exclusive, but mutually pervasive in a constant process of becoming. To accept this polarity is to accept humanity, but arbitrarily to make this polarity mutually exclusive and with equal arbitrariness to brand the one as good and the other as evil and then to maintain such "misplaced concreteness" with fanatical dogmatism is to deny humanity. But maybe the life-denying and the life-affirming attitudes are just another aspect of an all-pervasive polarity which is resolved in knowledge.

---

11. *Jnanasiddhi*, XV 16.
12. Ibid., XV 20.
13. Ibid., XV 14.
14. Ibid., XV 18.

20

*Just as a man and woman in close embrace know
nothing more of a without or a within, so also does
the Self embraced by the Spirit know nothing more of
a without or a within. This is the true Self in which
the whole of desire is satisfied.*

Brihadaranyaka Upanishad

SWAMI SIVANANDA RADHA

The Search for Union

One of the best-known tales of the Eastern spiritual tradition is that of Lord Krishna and his love affair with Radha
and the gopis. It is an enchanting and timeless story which
has inspired some of India's finest music, sculpture, paint-
ing, and poetry. Yet the deeper levels of its meaning are
revealed only to those who have embarked on their own
personal "love affair with the Divine," and who have become fluent in the language of symbolic interpretation. To
confuse spiritual metaphor with earthly reality is to miss
the essence of these beautiful teachings.

The gopis, young married women who tend the sacred
cows, are irresistibly drawn to follow the melody of Lord
Krishna's flute which is the inner call of the Most High. On
the strength of their love for the Divine, symbolized by the
youthful god, they forsake the security of home, family,

and worldly duties to follow their Lord. The gopis represent those seekers who attain Self-realization through intense devotion or bhakti, placing the longing for divine union before all other aspects of life. Krishna's attraction to the gopis is symbolic of divine acceptance and enjoyment of creation.

Radha, an incarnation of Cosmic Love, is the gopi chosen by Lord Krishna as his beloved. In her devotion and longing for Krishna, Radha symbolizes the human soul yearning for cosmic union with the oversoul. Her inspired prayer to the Lord is an expression of divine rather than physical love:

> O Thou, whom at first sight I knew for the Lord of my being and my God, receive my offering. Thine are all my thoughts, all my emotions, all the sentiments of my heart, all my sensations, all the movements of my life, each cell of my body, each drop of my blood. I am absolutely and altogether Thine, Thine without reserve. What Thou wilt of me that I shall be. Whether Thou choosest for me life or death, happiness or sorrow, pleasure or suffering, all that comes to me from Thee will be welcome. Each one of Thy gifts will be always for me a gift divine, bringing with it the supreme felicity
>
> The Mother

The legend tells how, after many fleeting encounters, attractions and repulsions, Radha and Krishna finally meet in sexual union in a secret grotto. In the account of their love-play or lila lies the secret of the cosmic dance between creation and unmanifest energy. It is the dynamic interaction between the Divine during creation toward realization, and creation luring the Divine toward experience.

This cosmic relationship is mirrored in human relations. The procreative function of sex links it inevitably to the cycle of human birth and death. It is impossible to give the "gift of life" without at the same time bestowing the experience of human suffering and death. Taking responsibility for a sexual relationship involves either the acceptance of possible parenthood or the choice to pay the price of effective birth control methods. A true spiritual union is one in which the partners have sufficient mental and emotional maturity to choose clearly whether or not to have children, and to accept the long-term responsibility for their decision. Those who decide to become parents must do so with full awareness of the demands involved and the potential tragedy of the world situation facing their children.

But lovers can develop a different understanding of physical union if they meditate together and dedicate the pleasures of their bodies to the Most High. Those who desire children can then offer themselves as guides and caretakers for the soul which may be born as a result of their union. They should take great joy in the offspring of their union, cherishing and respecting the child as a divine gift. This attitude toward children is very rare as it demands enormous control and selfless dedication for many years on the part of the parents.

To help the individual keep from slipping back under the control of the sexual instinct, which for many is an apparently uncontrollable force, there is a simple exercise from the Eastern spiritual tradition which offers much practical support for inner growth. The individual stands with an erect spine, and begins to walk around in as large a circle as space will permit, focusing attention on the chest. The arms are moved in a synchronized circular motion in front of the body, the lowest point of the circle being above the navel and the highest point above the head. The hands are extended with palms facing upward. While walking the individual repeats aloud in a firm strong voice: "I am functioning from my center." When practiced regularly for even five minutes each day, this exercise will bring about marvelous results in the cultivation of mental and emotional balance. Repetition of this affirmation leads to the generation of new understanding about the "pairs of opposites" of human existence, such as birth and death, love and hate, good and bad, God and the devil.

* * * * * * *

Another form of union occurs when two people enjoy something together independently of sex. This may come while experiencing the magnificence of nature such as the glory of a sunset, standing on the rim of the Grand Canyon, or viewing the mystery of living cells through a microscope. There can be union when two people together respond with awe and gratitude for works of art, sublime music, masterpieces of architecture. There is a meeting in joy as well as in sorrow which is itself a kind of joining on an emotional level.

Then there is the meeting of minds, seeing eye to eye with ideas that are created, each giving to the other spurts of energy as thoughts are communicated. Each person may experience increased creative inspiration as intuitive insights flow back and forth between them. These forms of union are all independent of sexual attraction yet, in the attraction of minds, ideas may be "fertilized by the union of thoughts."

Here we speak of kinds of unions that are different from the sexual one. When this possibility first enters a human mind, the person may begin to search for higher ideals and for a union that is not so fleeting and tied down with the creation of new beings. The notion that the only union is the sexual one, with its wrong emphasis on self-gratification, leads to an overload in the minds of people.

* * * * * * *

In the story of Radha and Krishna, the descriptions of their blissful lovemaking make no mention of offspring. Their union is not to be taken literally but is a divine metaphor for the merging of Cosmic Energy with its own creation. In order to truly appreciate the significance of a "love affair with the Divine," we must awaken to the promise that the bliss of spiritual union will surpass the pleasures of physical union.

At the moment of physical climax, a person may be absorbed totally in the experience and lose a sense of individuality for a few seconds. The yogis of old thought that such a blissful event was too short, and the price of repetition too high, incurring as it did a continuing responsibility to the partner and offspring. The choice of the yogi is to cultivate freedom—from the emotional and mental security found in a committed sexual relationship, from the desire for immortality through procreation, and from the responsibility for offspring. The challenge yoga presents is to devote all energy to the search for higher values in life, and to obtain the goal of spiritual bliss beyond the physical body.

We can look now into a form of union which is beyond concrete description—the union of the individual intelligence with Cosmic Intelligence. In ancient times, when the idea of this possibility first came into existence, there arose a dilemma. How could it be expressed so that it would be understood by those of different cultures and ages who would seek the higher values? The seers of old chose to communicate through concrete images of gods and goddesses in physical union. To the initiate these images meant much more than sexual intercourse—they stood for the union of the individual with Supreme Intelligence. But for the uneducated, they became a sign for them to indulge in their own gratification.

The adorned gods and goddesses have to be seen as concrete expressions of abstract ideals. The crowns on their heads are symbolic of the crowning state of consciousness and the intellect at its purest. It is through the five senses that life is known, and these sensory services which the body provides for the individual can take place on many levels from the very gross to the highly refined. It is no surprise that we find the sense organs of the gods and goddesses are bejewelled. The ear that listens is precious, the nose that can smell a divine presence is rare. The jewels show how refined and precious the senses of the deities have become.

As to the human body, it is capable of a great range of expression and experience from very gross perceptions and actions to those of the highest subtlety. The sexual energy which is used for self-gratification must be rechanneled in order to develop and refine the spiritual potential of the physical body. The seeker will discover that the body is capable of becoming a highly sensitive spiritual instrument. There are yogic exercises and practices which help refine the body into such a spiritual tool.

The claims of the sociobiologists that human beings are entirely controlled and manipulated by the commands of genetic inheritance do not apply to those individuals who have reached the level of awareness illuminated by the story of Radha and Krishna. It is an enormous struggle to break free from nature's insistence on the continuation of the human species. The path to higher consciousness and the goal of liberation from all impelling and compulsive forces exacts a high price in renunciation of human desires. Yet the way promises rewards of eternal value, far beyond the momentary pleasures of the physical body.

* * * * * * *

Human beings have created their own gods—Eros, money, science, political power. As long as humans breathe they will continue to create gods until these have outgrown their usefulness. And until the god of sex has outlived its usefulness it will continue its sensual pre-occupation, to rob the body and mind of its energy.

However, we can choose the way we live our life. The question of what kind of life we wish to pursue can be approached by this inquiry: "What kind of a person do I want to be"? The question is directed toward the physical levels which include sexuality, the mental levels which include the emotions, and the spiritual levels. Today, the former two levels receive undue attention, while spiritually people are starved. It is true that "misuse of anything brings its own punishment." A certain humility and a true desire to understand the divine laws will reveal that behind every such moral is an underlying law of manifestation which has been forgotten.

What choices are open to the individual who wishes to

become master of his or her own destiny? Can one become free of both external conditioning and internal compulsions? The transformation from the state of a human animal, content to eat, sleep, and procreate, to that of a fully "human" being begins with the recognition of the power of choice. It is up to each individual to decide the kind of person he or she wishes to become. In this time of spiritual need, it takes both courage and humility to seek an understanding of divine law, and to clarify personal ideals—of the body, the mind, the emotions, and the spirit. That clarification process is the first step in putting spiritual ideals into practice in all aspects of human life, including sexual relationships.

The defenders of the physical law—which make a religion out of self-gratification and turn sex into another god—miss the purpose of life. They should ask themselves if they were born for no other reason than to gain physical and sexual satisfaction. If that is so, man never would have risen above the animals, and the word *consciousness* would never have come into being. We have extended our sight with the telescope, our hearing with radar. Some people think that what can be experienced in sex can also be extended beyond its physical limitations.

The human being can be likened to a rainbow bridge between two worlds, the human and the divine. The path of liberation is open to anyone who recognizes that the other side of the rainbow is reachable. Those who desire to walk across the bridge must be willing to make the effort and pay the human price for the bliss of spiritual union.

*　*　*　*　*　*　*

In considering sex, love, and marriage from a yogic point of view, especially Kundalini Yoga, we see the latent energy in human beings which indicates that cooperation in their own evolution is a possibility for every man and woman. Like many systems, Kundalini has unfortunately undergone great deterioration and the clarity that has almost been lost can only be restored by a return to the old texts. There we will find to our great surprise that there is no reference to actual sexual relationships: the sexuality between gods and goddesses has to be understood as an interplay of forces. The only oneness that is fully known to most human beings is sexual intercourse because, at the moment of climax, there is for a few seconds the loss of individuality. This is to a small extent a state of bliss. For the yogis these flashes were not enough but they pointed to a possibility of bliss far greater than the physical experience.

Because of the interest in holistic medicine, Kundalini has recently come under scrutiny by psychologists. There has been much discussion as to what part Kundalini plays in the healing of the whole person. It should be understood, however, that it is usually emotional forces that make a person sick, and the releasing of these forces (which is also a sort of uncoiling—Kundalini means "coiled up") brings health. But this is not related to Kundalini.

If we made a general speculation about what Kundalini might be, we would describe it as the latent force which surfaces in geniuses such as Bach and Leonardo, and, in more recent times, Einstein.

Undoubtedly, great inspiration can arise to carry the human being beyond the commands of the genes. We can see this exemplified in masterpieces such as the Pantheon, Chartres, St. Peters, and other great works of art by creative geniuses like Michelangeo, Leonardo Da Vinci, Bach, and Mozart. Certainly, they must have had access to higher consciousness or Supreme Intelligence which created a great inspiration beyond the ordinary direction of genetic inheritance. For most people, however, inspiration lasts no longer than the light of the firefly that catches brief attention and then returns to the unknown. The question is, why are there not more people in the genius category?

The possibility that Kundalini could spontaneously arise in people and manifest itself in sexual energy has become a topic of wide interest. It has been used as an explanation or excuse for changes in sexual behavior, from simple modifications to excesses.

* * * * * * *

As well as the story of Radha and Krishna, with which we began our journey of investigation, there is another myth that can give us a clue to the yogic attitude to sex. This is the relationship of Siva and Parvati. The great renunciate, the great god Siva, being at one time overcome with longing for companionship, looked about and saw a young maiden who was engaged in perfect worship of him —the goddess, the devi, Parvati, and he longed to have her as a companion. Siva is the ascetic, the god who has his abode on Mt. Kailas where there is only snow and ice. Many Indians make a pilgrimage to Mt. Kailas once in a lifetime to attain great blessings. We are told that the god sits there in continuous unbroken meditation.

Yet this same Lord Siva is the god who danced in order to bring creation into existence. With each movement he brought another part of life into being. The dancing Siva is often shown in a wheel of fire, the fire of passion. Fire should not be seen only as a destructive force. With passionate intensity Siva danced his cosmic dance and created the world, but he could not dance alone. Siva symbolizes pure *unmanifest* energy; the energy that is *manifest* takes on a different aspect, symbolized by the female, Parvati. The cosmic dance of Siva and Parvati is like an elevated experience between two human beings.

But even the cosmic forces need rest. And even the Goddess Parvati (known also as Sakti and the Devi) cannot continuously create, for she too needs rest. The period of creation and the period of rest could represent eons of time. We must change our time concept in order to understand this. We call human time small time, calendar time, the years as they go by to make up the span of our lives. But Siva's time, the Devi's time, is great time—centuries, eons, cosmic time. This is taking time into a different dimension, far beyond even the astronomer's calculations of how long it takes for the light of a heavenly body to reach the earth and for us to see the stars.

Thinking in terms of great time, we can say that there is a cycle of creation in which this world is in existence. But one day a planet which is bustling with life will sink into oblivion and somewhere else life will burst forth again. It is possible that the moon may once have been a wonderful planet. Maybe some of the other stars and planets had life at one time. We do not know what has happened in these realms. The condensed energy in black holes may just be waiting once again to burst forth into a new manifestation, a new life cycle that may take another two or three million years until again a period of rest, of un-creation, will take place.

So Siva's time of rest or celibacy after the cosmic dance becomes the significant hint that human beings must also take rest. Jews and Christians have six days of work, one day of rest. Animal breeders do not mate their cattle every season. Even the fields should not be producing at all times but should be allowed to lie fallow at regular intervals.

Celibacy, or brahmacarya, and sexual activity are in contrast to each other, yet part of the same unit. But human sexuality has been exploited. One can only be dismayed at where man's preoccupation with sex has led him. Perhaps the ideas of Siva and Parvati can serve as a model for a completely new view.

The Mantra for the Muladhara Cakra in the Kundalini system expresses this concept beautifully:

> In the Muladhara of yours I worship Him who has nine natures, dancing the great Tandava, having nine sentiments, together with (His Sakti) Samaya, the quintessence of Lasya. It is from these two, each having its own presiding form, looking in compassion on the disposition of the origination (of the world) that this world has come into existence, having you as father and mother.

Commentary:

> Siva dances His Cosmic Dance, the Great Tandava
> Supreme Intelligence danced in the Self.

Siva and Sakti dance together, delicately blended.
    Rasa, the final awareness within.
The Center of being is touched, free from competition.
The great Tandava, the dramatic, the Cosmic
    activity, sometimes violent like a storm:
Lasya, the luring, the sweet, a whisper;
    move together in bliss, delight and
    timelessness, in perfect rhythm.
Through this dance the world comes into being.

In the play of the goddess (the devi), whose substance is consciousness, the dual principle of Siva/Sakti is presented as a male and female form, pointing to the polarity of the mind. Masculine and feminine principles are not narrowly limited, but are inseparable elements of energy giving birth to whirling worlds, from the tiny atom to millions of galaxies. Nothing fixed, nothing rigid. Richness in mystical variations expressing life itself.

The powers of mind and matter, creation and destruction, birth and death, are an interplay of forces embodied in the dance of Tandava-Lasya. In birth, death is hidden, as heat is hidden in fire. Illusion and desire dance together. Life is a Cosmic wave; dazzling creation. All forms come into existence upon the manifestation of consciousness.*

When Parvati became Siva's wife the other gods of the heavens would say, "What do you want with him, who has no place to offer you, who lives in ice and snow and takes the life of meditation?"

Parvati, the goddess of creation, somehow knew in her heart that there was more to the relationship. Her time with Siva would come. And from her dance with Siva, the world comes into being. Yet both alternate between times of creation and times of rest, asceticism and meditation. It seems to be that asceticism and meditation enhance the human being. The ascetic emanates a powerful attraction

---

*Swami Sivananda Radha. *Kundalini: Yoga for the West.* (Spokane, Wa.: Timeless Books), 1978.

to the opposite sex, as does a highly sexed individual. The average human being alternates between the two.

Married people would enhance their relationship by mutually agreeing to a period of celibacy from time to time. Sometimes a couple must take a rest or even a holiday away from each other. We must break habitual patterns such as the rationalization that "because we sleep in the same room, in the same bed, therefore we must have sex." Contrary to the ideas of the Freudian School of psychology, perhaps this idea is not healthy. As the goddess needs to take time in celibacy to renew her energy before she continues creation, so the woman watches and takes stock of what needs to be done, what changes are needed.

A couple that wants a lasting relationship would be wise to look at the attitude of the gods and goddesses. It is man's nature to be a seeder, to create, but man too needs intervals of inactivity. And sometimes that period of saving physical energy normally expended in sex can be of great importance. Anyone who interviews and counsels couples will know that exhausted people do not have the proper attitude toward sex. They have been brainwashed as to the importance of sex, as if we were born for nothing else. So we must re-establish true balance, and where can we obtain guidance? It is the great spiritual teachers who have pointed to the divine beings.

Today the world is overpopulated. There are very few tribes who need to worry about propagating their own species. Today we must take an attitude of discipline, especially in the Western world. As money is controlled through taxation and material is controlled through regulations, so people must self-regulate the number of offspring—before this too is dictated by government authority.

Intelligence does not need to be excluded from sex. Quality minimizes greed and quality can transform sexual life. The gods and goddesses can still speak to us through the old scriptures.

As we have to work on any good relationship, we have to work on the relationship in marriage. There are other values in life, other aspects to share beside our bodies. Preparation for the many facets of married life and the responsibilities of parenthood are inadequate without these considerations. Reality must balance romanticism if the marriage is to last.

Siva and Sakti engage in passionate love to create the world. They also engage in the passionate pursuit of rest, of meditation on their own creation—and so must we. We must not let ourselves be consumed by passionate sexual love, but by passionate love that expands into other areas of life. Each man and each woman, single or together, must decide what sex is going to mean in their lives. They must answer for themselves the questions that are asked in Kundalini yoga concerning the laying of the foundation by making a choice to direct the pure energy into other areas besides sex. Will it be used for creativity in the arts? What are the priorities?

We consider priorities in many areas of life. Now we have to include our sexual relationships, our sexual activities. The following of blind instincts is not fulfilling; rather it creates greed to have more and more indulgence because sex is not understood as a shifting of energies from one body to another, of each resonating in the other. What is considered sex in the average life can indeed be termed raw sex, raw instinctual gratification.

In understanding the steps that can be taken to elevate sex, we can classify people into several stages. Primitive man has little understanding of what sex is, but in the second stage there may come an awareness, a half-knowledge of what sex is all about and perhaps a different choice of partners.

In the third stage the awakening of sex may be for gratification and exploitation, yet there is a dawning in the mind and heart that sexual activity will turn into sexual love. Demands are much less, accommodating the partner becomes more frequent. The question is asked, what is sex all about? Since at a certain age the woman can no longer produce offspring, is sex only for procreation? If so, why would the attraction of sex and the experience of sexual activity not stop at that time? Perhaps sexual relationships have their different phases too. We should not rule this out. For many couples passionate sex life will come only when they are freed from the possibility of offspring. Then sex takes on an increased experience of love, to expand into greater understanding of love that is inclusive of sex. However, the needed rest period must not be forgotten, must not be left out. The occasional glass of wine, the exceptional gourmet meal will only remain something special when its value is not diluted by daily habit.

Love in marriage can be renewed by assigning times of celibacy. This may be for three months or a year or two, to renew strength, to renew energy, also to give the opportunity to delve deep within, coming to understand self, continuing the process of growth to wholeness, to all-round development. The yogic system provides this: Hatha Yoga brings the physical to a higher level to psychological and mystical aspects; Bhakti Yoga, love and devotion, looked down upon often by the intellectual who has not enough understanding of what love really is to appreciate the benefits; Jnana Yoga, wisdom, the yoga of understanding, of understanding the mind. These together make up the Kingly Yoga. The Gita points to 18 types of yoga. Each couple can choose their own and practice parts of it together.

What would your relationship, your togetherness, mean if you would meditate before engaging in sex? Perhaps you would become indeed aware of the finer forces that are also called into existence by a different attitude to sex and by an exchange of energy, currents that flow between two bodies. What would it mean if you would meditate after you have experienced sexual bliss—to continue to let that burst into Divine Light, into Light that could only be called of a divine nature, something that moves your whole being?

A marvelous adventure for Western man lies ahead. For too long he has been kept in the dark and given false promises. We cannot all be great yogis, mini-Sivas, but we can still bring quality into all aspects of our lives and make sex meaningful in love, and sex and love meaningful in a marriage that flowers and inspires others to flower also.

Here is a list of authors whose essays appear in
A Spiritual Approach to Male/Female Relations
and who have also written other Quest books—

Claude Bragdon
>   The Beautiful Necessity

Gina Cerminara
>   Insights for the Age of Aquarius

Haridas Chaudhuri
>   Being, Evolution and Immortality
>   The Evolution of Integral Consciousness
>   Integral Yoga
>   Mastering the Problems of Living

Clara Codd
>   The Ageless Wisdom of Life
>   Trust Yourself to Life

J. Krishnamurti
>   Commentaries on Living, Series I, II, and III

Geddes MacGregor
>   The Christening of Karma
>   The Gospels as a Mandala of Wisdom
>   Reincarnation in Christianity

Dane Rudhyar
>   The Astrology of Transformation
>   Beyond Individualism
>   Culture, Crisis and Creativity
>   Occult Preparations for a New Age
>   The Rhythm of Wholeness

Jay Williams
>   Judaism
>   Yeshua Buddha

These titles are available from:
The Theosophical Publishing House
306 W. Geneva Rd., Wheaton, IL 60189